SOCIAL
SELLING
MASTERY

SOCIAL SELLING MASTERY

MASTERY

SCALING UP YOUR SALES
AND MARKETING MACHINE
FOR THE DIGITAL BUYER

JAMIE SHANKS

WILEY

Library of Congress Cataloging-in-Publication Data:

Names: Shanks, Jamie, author.
Title: Social selling mastery : scaling up your sales and marketing machine
    for the digital buyer / Jamie Shanks.
Description: Hoboken, New Jersey : John Wiley & Sons, Inc., [2016] | Includes
    index.
Identifiers: LCCN 2016023352 (print) | LCCN 2016031884 (ebook) |
    ISBN 9781119280736 (cloth) | ISBN 9781119280767 (epdf) |
    ISBN 9781119280866 (epub)
Subjects: LCSH: Internet marketing. | Selling. | Electronic commerce. |
    Social media.
Classification: LCC HF5415.1265 .S525 2016 (print) | LCC HF5415.1265 (ebook)
    | DDC 658.8/72—dc23
LC record available at https://lccn.loc.gov/2016023352

Printed in the United States of America.

10 9 8 7 6 5 4 3 2 1

Contents

PART FOUR
Scaling Up with Sales Operations and
Sales Enablement   169

Preface

My life changed forever on April 18, 2012, in Dallas, Texas. On that particular day, I was a first-time attendee to the AA-ISP (American Association of Inside Sales Professionals) annual Leadership Summit. I was the Toronto AA-ISP chapter president at the time, yet hadn't been able to attend the 2011 event because I had absolutely no money. That year was a disastrous one for my business, which you'll feel a true appreciation for by the end of this preface. At the 2012 AA-ISP Leadership Summit, I felt like a fish out of water. There, at this event, were all the big names of inside sales—Anneke Seley, Trish Bertuzzi, Ken Krogue, Jill Konrath, and hundreds more. Then there was me, from Canada, a 33-year-old absolute nobody in the industry. I remember feeling really awkward at the event because I was there to learn, but I also was very starstruck. My heroes have always been business leaders and now I was in a room with the top sales minds in the world. I kept saying to myself, "I'm meeting the people whose books are on my book shelf at home." I just wanted someone to pay attention to me.

To better understand my sense of desperation at the time, I'll paint you a picture of my financial dire straits. I'll take the story back three more years, to the summer of 2009. In that year, I was a self-proclaimed, hot-shit sales leader who made magic happen every time I picked up the phone. I was convinced that I was wasting my talents leading one sales team as an employee when I could be consulting to 10 at the same time as an entrepreneur. On January 4, 2010, I quit my job as the director of sales at Firmex (a SaaS software start-up in Toronto) and became a consultant. The first thing I learned about consulting is that there are zero barriers to entry, but 99 reasons why you'll fall flat on your face! I convinced myself that local Toronto technology companies would flock to my greatness. I'll spare you 18 months of terrible stories, but suffice it to say, I had a failing business that couldn't seem to turn a profit. I kept asking myself, "Why is my business such a disaster?" The answers to my problematic start were only clear to me years later:

1. As a self-proclaimed sales expert, I didn't eat my own dog food. I didn't develop my sales pipeline every single day.
2. I had no idea how to properly manage cash flow for a business. I must have slept through cash-flow analysis in MBA school!
3. I didn't create a personal brand. The telephone is great for quick hits, but by 2011 business leaders were already taking to the Internet to answer questions to their problems. I was nowhere to be found!

Nearly two years after starting my business, in March 2011, I was teetering on the edge of bankruptcy. Then, like a slap in the face from sales karma, three days before my wedding, the bomb dropped! I went to visit my top-billing client at the company's office and the doors were locked. I came to find out that certain executives of this company had committed fraud by illegally sucking money out of the corporation. All non-equity-owning C-level executives, the employees, and unsecured contractors got screwed overnight! As an unsecured contractor, my business was never going to get paid. I was owed $35,000, but with the state of my financial affairs, it might as well have been $100,000,000. I was dead! I had little backfill of clients to support this mounting debt and I was leaving for Costa Rica for my wedding, and then to Paris, France, for our honeymoon in just three . . . freaking . . . days! There was no way I was telling my soon-to-be wife what had just happened, as I assumed if I did, that this marriage thing would be over before it even began.

After returning home from an amazing, but very expensive, wedding and honeymoon, reality sunk in. I came back to a rainy Toronto in late March 2011 only to fully grasp the devastation to my business. I was faced with laying off all my employees, not paying myself for two months, and no real prospects to help my family survive. I was scared, so scared that I felt like vomiting nearly every day. I was in desperation mode, one of several moments that will define what kind of person you are. Many entrepreneurs around the world have had very similar moments like mine, and many times, their best eureka moments are sparked from desperation. My eureka moment ignited a second-half comeback that warrants me telling you this story to help set the stage for this book.

Throughout the summer of 2011, I worked to support my few remaining clients, but was preoccupied with thinking about new business development for myself. At night, every night, many times at 3 a.m., I would be in our spare bedroom, staring aimlessly at my laptop, hoping that some serendipitous event would come save my business. I can vividly remember these nights like a recurring bad dream. Oddly enough, I would have LinkedIn open on the home page. I honestly don't remember why LinkedIn specifically. I would spend hours and hours thinking about all my business development success via the telephone, and thought about how I could communicate with prospective buyers faster and with greater scale. This speed-to-market thinking is what probably had me staring at LinkedIn. I began to really see the potential of LinkedIn as it seemed like I was one-degree connection away from so many Toronto vice presidents of sales. Unfortunately, I couldn't find best practices online to help me monetize LinkedIn. I remember thinking about my experiences via the telephone, and kept trying to mentally reverse-engineer my process inside LinkedIn. Slowly, throughout the summer of 2011, I started to figure out new ways to create sales opportunities for myself on LinkedIn. Each time I had successful breakthrough the night before, the next morning I would show my existing clients the tactics I had used. I found that clients were more excited to learn my LinkedIn sales tactics than to talk about my existing sales consulting services. Week by week, month by month, I got better and better at monetizing the powers of LinkedIn. Not only was I becoming effective with the tool, but my clients were showing repeatable success and quantifiable return-on-effort from my tips. By autumn of 2011, the entrepreneurial lightbulb turned on in my head—"If only I could find a way to turn my new LinkedIn sales tactics into a business."

Fast forward to the afternoon of April 18, 2012, at the AA-ISP Leadership Summit in Dallas, Texas. At the conference, there was a breakout session by Josiane Fegion titled "Wake Up and Press Refresh on Social Media." When I first arrived at the conference, I noticed this session on the agenda, and preplanned that this would be my moment to speak up in front of the entire room about my LinkedIn tactics. As I walked into the breakout room, I took a seat in the middle of the room on the right side. Little did I know, I was surrounded by sales and marketing superstars:

- Left of me: Gary Ambrose—CEO of TimeTrade
- Right of me: Ralf VonSosen—then CMO of InsideView, later to become CMO of LinkedIn Sales Solutions
- Behind me: Ken Krogue—Co-Founder of InsideSales.com

About 10 minutes into Josiane's presentation, she asked the audience for specific examples of sales success leveraging social media. I sprung up like a leopard looking to attack a gazelle! I shouted "We have been helping clients send LinkedIn InMail to prospects with a 12- to 20-percent message-sent-to-new-lead-created ratio." That one line changed my life forever. Honestly, I can pinpoint the moment exactly. The breakout room's temperature seemed to change as the buzzing of chatter began to build. People looked at me as though I had invented fire. Almost immediately, someone from the back had shouted, "Can you describe exactly what you're doing on LinkedIn?" So, for the next few moments, I explained what I later would call the sphere of influence sales process. I felt like a rock star for the first time in my life. I had potentially created a consulting service that people actually wanted!

After the breakout session had finished, Gary Ambrose and Ken Krogue approached me to exchange business cards. They both asked me to call them to discuss doing a joint webinar and ebook on the topic of LinkedIn. I walked into the main lobby of the conference center with a sense of hope and newly found self-confidence I hadn't felt in two years. The very next thing I did was call my business partner George Albert. This call should have been recorded, and I should plaster its text on the walls of our corporate office:

Jamie: "George, it's Jamie."

George: "How is the conference, any great leads?"

Jamie: "George . . . I'm telling you, we're scrapping everything! I have been talking about our LinkedIn stuff, and people around here are calling it 'Social Selling.' George, we're going to stop all of our other services and just coach people on Social Selling!"

George: "Are you f&%king mental?"

George may tell you this isn't exactly what he said, but I beg to differ. He was right: How could we dismantle a business that was slowly starting to climb out of the abyss for this social selling thing? But for me, the point was simple, as s*ocial selling* was a term that only a few people on earth could define. But, it seemed the appetite to solving this social media for sales thing was only going to grow exponentially.

Throughout the summer of 2012, I began to test my assumptions on the demand for social selling. George and I agreed that I would create a basic curriculum and train ten clients for free! Based on their feedback and quantitative success, we would both have a sense for the demand, and we would have ten client success stories to shop to future buyers. Providing our training for free was one of the smartest business ideas I've ever executed. Within 90 days, we had ten extremely satisfied advocates and collected empirical sales success from these engagements.

I guess you can say, the rest is history. Over the next four years, we've created the world's largest social selling training system called Social Selling Mastery. As of the date of this publication, our system is being used by more than 60,000 sales and marketing professionals worldwide, and growing exponentially. We've helped companies acquire billions of dollars of incremental sales pipeline and revenue. It's been incredible to see our curriculum on every continent, in every size of company, within dozens of industries. Our idea of giving free training to our first customers in exchange for feedback inspired us to crowdsource all future curriculum development. Our current curriculum, the basis for this book, is the most robust and comprehensive in the world because it's consistently evolving from sales and marketing professionals' feedback.

I want to share my humble social selling beginnings with you because it proves that anyone can build a personal brand. Building a personal brand is going to be a major step you'll take to scale your company in this new digital economy. If you and your entire sales and marketing organization apply the principles based in this book, I promise you that social selling will positively affect the growth trajectory of your company. I can't wait to hear your stories of social selling success!

—Jamie Shanks

Acknowledgments

This book would not exist without my beautiful wife, Rebecca Shanks. Her contributions go well beyond this publication, as I wouldn't have a business without her. Rebecca ensured my survival as an entrepreneur as both the household matriarch and financial stabilizer.

We're blessed with two incredible children, Hunter and Henley Shanks. I can't fully articulate how much of what I do is to better serve them. I once read that a parent's job is to become a series of positive memories for his or her children. This is what excites me about this book. My children (ages four and two at the time of publication) will know the successes that entrepreneurship has brought our family, but this book serves as a memory of how hard Rebecca and I worked to achieve that success.

The foundation to my work ethic is from my parents. While they're not entrepreneurs themselves, they work harder than anyone I know. They also supported me in every hare-brained business idea I've ever had. The lesson I've learned is that you must allow your children to freely choose their own path, no matter how different from your own. My parents let me experiment, and they let me fall down. I believe entrepreneurs can be grown and cultivated from a very young age. I was one of those lucky people.

My closest friends, Mitch, Travis, and George, and my brother, Casey, and sister, Shannon, have been through the entrepreneurship battle with me for decades. They are incredible sounding boards, and I love them for it.

Finally, this book is fueled by Sales for Life and the amazing culture that George Albert and I have helped create. Our fast-growing team is committed to owning social and digital selling globally—and that all starts with fostering a culture that helps innovation thrive.

Introduction: The Road Map to Digital Transformation

Definition of synergy: The whole is greater than the sum of its parts.

—Aristotle

I use Aristotle's definition of synergy to outline your road map to a digital transformation inside your organization. I can't stress this enough: Social selling success is a team sport, not a showcase for great individual contributions. Great teams that act as one cohesive unit always win more championships than the teams that gather amazing individual talent on paper. If there are only a few anecdotes that you remember from this book, please remember this definition of synergy and how teamwork is always going to outperform individuals working in a vacuum.

Every organization, no matter how effective at traditional selling principles, will start its digital transformation from simple beginnings. For hundreds of technology companies in San Francisco, this evolution has already happened, but for many global financial services companies, the seeds have just been planted. No matter where your company is in the process, all companies will face the digital transformation in six stages. The question you must ask yourself is: Where is my organization in this progression?

LEVEL 0: STATUS QUO

Your organization is complacent and will continue selling as it always has. You have not established with your sales team the mindset that social and digital communication will have a positive impact on the business. There is little to no buy-in from commercial leaders on the effectiveness of social media, no social governance, and no formal training on social selling. The adage "sales is from Mars; marketing is from Venus" couldn't be more true. These two departments couldn't be more disconnected. Is this your organization, one in which sales and marketing barely speak? Are they even located in the same building, city, or country?

LEVEL 1: RANDOM ACTS OF SOCIAL

"Random acts of social" is a popularized term by PeopleLinx. The social seed has been planted somewhere in your organization, but it hasn't gone viral. Pockets of individuals, typically high-performing sales professionals, are attempting to create a groundswell of change. The problem with this is that there's little to no empirical evidence to support the effectiveness of social media in sales. While a few commercial leaders may believe in social strategies, your corporate sales approach is pretty much status quo. Social selling is a whisper throughout the halls of your sales and marketing departments.

LEVEL 2: BUILDING A BUSINESS CASE: LINKEDIN OR SOCIAL MEDIA TRAINING

At this stage, your organization has had enough internal demand for social best practices that someone is trying to formalize a game plan, and build a business case. In spite of this, it's likely that you or your teammates have confused LinkedIn and social selling as one and the same. As a result, you've probably made any of these investments:

- *Multiple LinkedIn Sales Navigator licenses.* Your department's sales tool stack needed to standardize a LinkedIn product.
- *Training workshops.* Someone at your company was chosen to facilitate training. (Cue the social media marketer or a digitally native sales professional who seems to *get it.*)

Your sales enablement team is trying to gather ideas for a "Social Selling 101" workshop filled with a basic assortment of tips, tricks, and tactics. You and your sales team will learn the basics of becoming social, starting with redesigning your social profiles. Unfortunately, these training workshops are usually two missing ingredients: first, a road map to global change beyond these initial workshops to enable you to measure success; second, the involvement of marketing in this social selling equation, as the sales team is not being fueled with new insights to share with your customers.

LEVEL 3: SCALE: SOCIAL SELLING MASTERY

Your Social Selling Mastery organization has top-down executive support to make social a priority. Your frontline sales leaders are driving accountability throughout their sales force to ensure social actions are reaching the defined measurable milestones. The digital marketing team is working side by side with sales to fuel the insights (i.e., content) that sales professionals will use to engage their buyer.

Social selling is manifesting beyond a business unit and seeking to be standardized throughout your entire sales and marketing organization. To become a Social Selling Mastery company, you understand that social selling effectiveness is not accomplished through a few training workshops. You and your sales enablement team will seek to weave social media into the DNA of your existing sales process. Social selling is additive, not a replacement for how your team sells today. You'll also ensure the skill gap between existing sales professionals and future new hires is nonexistent by making social-selling training part of your new hire onboarding.

Throughout all business units, your sales and marketing teams are leveraging social "every deal, every day" (to borrow a phrase from Jill Rowley) as part of the following three intersecting pillars of social selling:

1. *Trigger-based selling:* Internal or external events happening around your buyer. This digital information can alert a sales professional in real time, allowing for highly contextual conversations.
2. *Insights-based selling:* According to Forrester and Corporate Visions, "74% of buyers choose the sales team that was first to provide value and insight within their buying journey." Shaping your buyer's journey early is critical, and leveraging digital insights will help arm your buyer with information to make informed decisions.
3. *Referral-based selling:* People buy from people. The road map of relationships can be mechanized through tools such as LinkedIn and Twitter. You can build a relationship road map to establish deeper connections with your buyer.

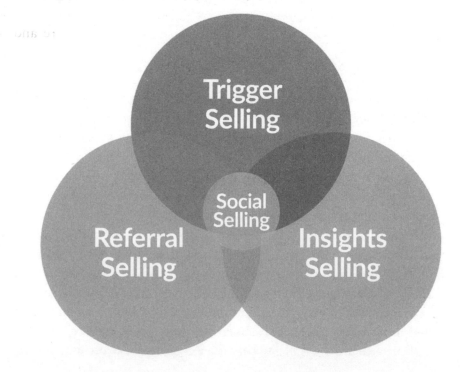

LEVEL 4: SALES AND MARKETING ALIGNMENT

Social selling is simply a by-product of effective sales and marketing alignment at scale across your organization. We've met companies that have renamed their social selling initiatives "digital sales," as they recognize that digital communication goes far beyond social platforms such as LinkedIn. These companies have created streamlined communication bridges between sales and marketing, which has increased the flow of new ideas for digital insights. At a tactical level, your company would have an Insights Committee, which is a group of sales professionals that meets regularly with the marketing department to develop new digital insights that fuel sales conversations. This consistently developed intellectual property (IP) is repeated by creating a process that we call the *IP Transfer Loop*. The IP Transfer Loop has a sales professional story-tell an idea based on buyers' challenges, then the marketing team turns this idea into a new digital insight for sales professionals to leverage with their buyers. As the sales team deploys these digital insights into the market, buyers provide more feedback in the form of objections, concerns, and questions. This cycle continues to repeat itself, with more sales feedback, while developing more and more granular insights that are highly valuable for the buyer.

Sales and marketing alignment also begins to formulate new ways to measure success. Great social selling teams recognize that a buyer's journey involves both the marketing and sales efforts; thus, everyone in marketing and sales becomes accountable to winning that new buyer. You'll recognize greater sales and marketing alignment when your marketing team is no longer focusing on website traffic or lead volumes as their ultimate key metric. Alignment occurs when your team begins to create metrics around the handshake between sales and marketing, which can mean sales-qualified leads or another metric at the opportunity level. Marketing will be accountable for delivering a percentage of sales-qualified leads to achieve a sales professional's quota attainment, while sales will be accountable for the timely pursuit and proper nurturing of these leads with social selling best practices. Everyone is ultimately responsible for new sales bookings. Tactically, a service-level agreement between sales and marketing takes form and becomes the blueprint for accountability among all team members.

LEVEL 5: SALES AND MARKETING INTEGRATION

As a Level 5 organization, you firmly believe that integration between sales and marketing is the future of commercial interactions with your buyer. *Team Revenue* is what we call the interlaced marketing and sales departments. Your commercial team recognizes emphatically that everyone in digital marketing and sales is accountable for helping buyers throughout their journey. All team members have completely bought into Aristotle's definition of *synergy*; they acknowledge that no role is more important than another; and understand that there are no short-cuts to becoming a successful digital-sales organization. We recognize that while the business cards and LinkedIn profiles of sales and market-ers will always show the external world their traditional roles and titles, internally it is clear that they are all members of one unit—Team Revenue. They are accountable to only one number—sales bookings!

Throughout this book, we explore very tactical steps to help you reach beyond even Level 3—Social Selling Mastery—so you can create greater collaboration between sales and marketing. I truly dream of a day when I see joint sales and marketing conferences, where both sales and marketing professionals are attending equally, collaborating and trading best practices as if they all share a common role. I also dream of the day when marketers have as much involvement in sales kick-off events (SKOs) by working hand in hand with sales to better address customer needs. Sales and marketing integration is coming, mark my words. Social Selling Mastery is going to be your company's biggest leap forward on the journey to integration.

We at Sales for Life have trained more than 250 companies, ranging in size from 5 sales and marketing professionals to 25,000 spread across the globe. Personally, I've been in more than 1,000 boardrooms (virtually or live) to assess companies' elementary starts to Social Selling at Levels 0, 1, and 2.

After reviewing the six stages to digital transformation, please don't get discouraged if your self-assessment places your organization far, far, far away from trying Level 3, Social Selling Mastery. This book is going to serve as your guide and road map.

HOW DO I USE THIS BOOK?

I have taken two very deliberate steps in creating this book for you:

1. This book is very tactical.

I want you and your organization to have the road map to social selling success. You're going to notice very quickly that we spend little time making the case for social selling in your organization. The *why* has been beaten to death; there are hundreds of articles online available for your review. My assumption is that you've purchased this book because your organization is stuck at Level 1 or Level 2 and you need the road map to Level 3, Social Selling Mastery. I promise you one thing: This book is very tactical and applies to both an individual, quota-carrying sales professional, all the way to a senior C-level executive rolling out a global training program. I will have accomplished my goal for this book if you feel it becomes your bible for social selling. You're getting a brain dump of four years of expertise with hundreds of customer engagements and an outline of best practices from Sales for Life. I legitimately want to change your life and the success trajectory of your organization.

2. Social selling at Scale

Scale—this is the missing ingredient of every book and training program claiming to be on social selling I've encountered. Their programs have done an admirable job of helping sales professionals kick-start their social selling activities. Unfortunately, they haven't approached social selling as a global initiative, littered with the complexities of multiple departmental stakeholders, training deliverables that reinforce behavioral change, and global KPI measurements that drive a real sales impact to your company's bottom line. Social selling execution based on the individual sales professional's activities is like sailing a ship without a course. Based on an independent study conducted by Feedback Systems with over 300 sales professionals with insight from Sales for Life, PeopleLinx, Sales Readiness Group, VorsightBP, and Sandler Training, we found that 69 percent of social sellers were self-taught, with no formal training, and they couldn't bottle their process.[1] These pockets of successful social sellers could hardly articulate what made their process so special. The problem this poses for your organization is simple: Core performers (typically 50 to 70 percent of your sales force) are not executing the same playbook as your high performers. According to the Corporate Executive Board, "Boosting Core Performers' sales performance by 5% will result in a 60% higher increase in revenue, than firms that increase their High Performers' sales performance by 5%."[2] This statement is obvious when you factor in the importance of scale. This is exactly why you need to look at social selling as part of a synergistic ecosystem. In keeping with this approach, all elements of this book are equally important; they are not just tips for sales professionals to execute in their own vacuum. This book has designed a daily sales cadence for every sales professional in your organization. There are also key steps for frontline sales managers, sales operations and sales enablement, and digital marketing. All of these business units must learn, execute, and measure in unison.

Before you dig in, here's an important tip: Don't skip sections, even if they're not part of your current job description. While this book is organized by job-function sections, please read each section in detail. I wrote each section to speak directly to the leader of that applicable job function. If you're in a part that doesn't align to your current role, **still**

---

[1] Sales for Life. "The State of Social Selling in 2016," blog post, December 9, 2015. Available at: http://www.salesforlife.com/blog/infographics/the-state-of-social-selling-in-2016-infographic/

[2] Corporate Executive Board. "Six Myths of Sales Performance," blog post, July 26, 2010. Available at: https://www.cebglobal.com/blogs/six-myths-of-sales-performance/.

read it. Read that part and its applicable chapters as if you were the leader. The only way you'll become the ultimate social seller is if you understand how the entire ecosystem works in unison. I'd like you to gain an appreciation for how each department is critical for social selling success.

One

CREATING A MINDSET SHIFT FOR A DIGITAL TRANSFORMATION

CHAPTER 1

Why Do I Need to Change Now, Not Tomorrow?

90% of customer buying decisions are starting online.
—2011 by Forrester Research

The above statistic is already five years old, but it couldn't be truer. The average buyer in business is just like you and me at night, on our couch, surfing the Internet. Buyers purchase clothes and televisions, and build their future vehicles online. What makes you think they don't also research software, HR best practices, insurance, or corporate health-care policies?

My business, our clients' businesses, and your business have already forever changed because buyers have changed. Buyers are arming themselves with more information than ever to make informed decisions. They can now connect with their peers on social platforms such as LinkedIn, Twitter, and Facebook to learn about the challenges, pitfalls, and successes of any solution implementation. In 2012, other statistics began to emerge on the change in buyers' behavior that progressed social selling:

- Fifty-seven percent of the buyer's journey takes place before a sales professional is involved.[1]
- Seventy-five percent of business-to-business (B2B) buyers use social media to research vendors.[2]

In 2011 and 2012, these core statistics awakened progressive companies because their sales professionals saw the vital importance that social media played during activity at the top of the sales funnel. Sales and marketing departments would need to change their ways to become resources for buyers *before* a sales professional would even know an opportunity existed. I can personally count dozens of clients over the last four years who attracted bluebirds (B2B clients) into their sales pipeline through social. At first, I would chalk up these seemingly serendipitous opportunities to great fortune, but it has become very clear that providing value to someone has been the catalyst. In May 2012, Aberdeen Group presented a finding about social sellers: "79% of sales professionals achieved quota in their last calendar fiscal year, compared to the 58% non–Social Sellers who were Average to Laggard in their industry. This had a 16.3% increase in their companies' overall revenue."[3] Such empirical evidence was hard to ignore.

In 2013, Craig Elias, the author of *Shift*, presented me with this mind-blowing statistic from Forrester: "74% of buyers are choosing the sales professional and company that was **first** to add value and

---

[1] Corporate Executive Board (CEB), 2012.Blog, March 31, 2015, https://www.cebglobal.com/blogs/b2b-sales-and-marketing-two-numbers-you-should-care-about/

[2] International Data Corporation, IDC Social Business Study, February 2014, https://business.linkedin.com/content/dam/business/sales-solutions/global/en_US/c/pdfs/idc-wp-247829.pdf

[3] Aberdeen Group, https://business.linkedin.com/content/dam/business/sales-solutions/global/en_US/site/pdf/ti/linkedin_social_selling_impact_aberdeen_report_us_en_130702.pdf

insight in the buying journey."[4] What does that mean? It means that long before you think about adding value for a prospective buyer via phone, email, or presentation, the buyer has been learning without you. Buyers have been collecting enough information to be able to select which vendors are best for their business. They do all this before ever speaking to a sales professional. Then, as buyers make decisions about vendors, they typically choose the first one who presented them with new ideas, concepts, and road maps. This is scary because all this education is happening without you! Your competition has been teaching your prospective buyers with their blogs, videos, infographics, ebooks, webinars, and success stories. Your buyers are shifting their priorities before you've even called them for the first time. Think about this scenario: You're about to conduct a huge presentation in the buyer's boardroom. You've been preparing statistics, ROI calculations, and reasons why your company is the best vendor for the project. The problem is that when you start your presentation, it doesn't go anything like what you planned in your mind. The client seems completely educated on your market—the features, implementation strategies, best practices, and pricing. In fact, the flow of the conversation seems like a grand inquisition, as the buyer has been prepped with landmine-like questions. Guess what? I, the social seller, was the one who set up those landmines! I, the social seller, had been sharing best practices, implementation road maps, and pricing scenarios to the buyer for months. The buyer now uses my solution as the benchmark and, because I taught him or her all the pitfalls to look out for, your solution seems to feel like it's been *sold* into the business, rather than being a right fit. While this is a simplistic description of social sellers impact, this is how social media affects buyers—and you.

It's time to take an objective look at your business. Has it become more difficult to reach decision-makers over the phone or via email? Are these time-tested ways of reaching out having the same effect they did even a few years ago? Also, the *buyer* is not just one person anymore.

---

[4] Forrester, January 27, 2014, http://blogs.forrester.com/mark_lindwall/14-01
-27-to_win_against_increasing_competition_equip_your_salespeople_with_a_
deeper_understanding_of_your_buy

According to the CEB, "There are now on average 5.4 decision-makers, champions and influencers, all part of the buying decision."[5] Are you effectively nurturing and influencing these five or six champions, influencers, and decision-makers in the organization with the phone? This is another reason social media has become a tool for sales professionals. With one article shared socially, I'm able to educate and become a resource to an account's 5.4 decision-makers—and thousands of others—instantly. This kind of scale is unmatched by the phone or email.

In 2014, LinkedIn did a study of 5,000 buyers in leadership positions and found that "92% of buyers want to deal with the sales professional who is the known thought-leader in their industry versus 17% of buyers who still don't mind being cold called."[6] By 2015, a new analysis had emerged: 34 percent of all B2B researchers are Millennials.[7] While the decision-maker might be a Gen Xer or Baby Boomer, the functional users and champions who support buying trends are digital natives.

Where does this leave you and your organization if you're not leading the customer conversation? You're a ghost, lost in a sea of screaming voices. What is the probability that you'll be found? You are working at a Fortune 2000 company and, for a brief moment, roll your eyes and think, "This doesn't apply to me. I work at XYZ Company, and we have a brand as the market leader." If this is your reaction, your future is in even more trouble! At a macro level, Forrester studies suggest that one million sales roles will be wiped out by 2020. These declining roles will be order takers (decline by 37 percent); explainers, sales professionals who demo (down 27 percent); and navigators, relationship-nurturing sales professionals (down 17 percent). All these roles are reduced because they do not present a face for the industry. You're not the consultant shaping the buyer's journey; you're only answering questions along the way. At a micro, personal level, people who work at a big

---

[5] CEB, October 22, 2014, https://www.cebglobal.com/blogs/sales-why-you-should-teach-customers-how-to-buy/
[6] LinkedIn, 2014. September 30, 2014, https://business.linkedin.com/sales-solutions/blog/t/the-most-important-bar-graph-youll-see-all-year
[7] May 11, 2015, http://www.pewresearch.org/fact-tank/2015/05/11/millennials-surpass-gen-xers-as-the-largest-generation-in-u-s-labor-force/

business are not very nimble. They can't start guerilla marketing campaigns like their smaller competitors.

Don't think for a moment that because of your business card, you're an obvious vendor choice. People buy from people *first;* then they buy into the solutions that a person represents. Your corporate business card might get you a few more meetings than competitors at smaller companies but, many times, the value ends there. Nimble, smaller competitors can unleash ground-breaking insights that disrupt your sales cycles. Now your buyer is armed and dangerous with market information, so how are you going to stand out? Why do they need you?

If an information technology or telecommunications company is not executing social selling at global level in 2016, it's no longer an early innovator—they're late to the party. As LinkedIn mentioned at its 2015 SalesConnect event in Las Vegas, 2016 to 2020 will be about *crossing the chasm* for many technology-focused companies. For those of you in other industries such as professional services, health care, finance, or manufacturing, your markets are changing rapidly! This isn't a scare tactic, but a reality check.

You need to change your mindset more about social selling's involvement beyond the sales role. How are sales operations, sales enablement, and, especially, marketing influencing your digital interactions with buyers? The size and scale of your organization is irrelevant here. Throughout this book, we'll use the word *global* as a ubiquitous term for *all* of your organization. What's most important is that you change your mindset from *me* activity to *we* activity, taking a global view. *We* is only important if it improves your entire organization's ability to serve your buyers. *That's it!* Nothing else matters with social selling or any type of innovative sales process. Your sales approach must have a positive impact on your ability to enhance your buyer's experience. I've seen B2C (business-to-consumer) companies change their digital approach years ago to enhance a buyer's experience. Unfortunately, B2B (business-to-business) companies have been approaching social selling as a series of individually executed sales *hacks* to create quick wins, but they have done little to improve long-term trust within their buyer-to-seller interactions.

I know it's hard to think of the long game here. I get it: You're measured with monthly or quarterly goals that make it difficult to think about your commercial approach two, three, five years from now. You're looking for a material impact to be made this quarter, and social selling tips, tricks, and tactics will book you immediate meetings and create quick opportunities. I can relate to this directly because it is how Sales for Life started its social selling training in 2012. But I promise you, the metaphor that constantly pops into my head will hold true: Picture a massive wave approaching your dam, which represents your company. As your buyers leverage social and digital media to make informed buying decisions, it becomes clear that the wave is inevitability going to hit your dam. Your approach to mending your cracking dam is using social media *hacks*. This is like using concrete filler for the cracks in the dam. These tips, tricks, and tactics can keep your dam together for the short term, but the engineer in you knows you're doomed if you don't find a long-term, scalable solution. Please don't throw up your hands and say, "That's not my job." Perhaps you can't fix the dam alone, but don't dismiss your ability to be a change agent for the construction of an entirely new structure. You bought this book to help give your company a road map and playbook to social selling and, within the book, we help you identify the key players necessary for success within your company. The key takeaway here is that social media tips, trick, and tactics, when used within tools such as LinkedIn, are great at establishing buy-in for social selling. But you're not reading this book for buy-in, you want a global Social Selling Mastery program that scales beyond a few high-performing sales professionals. If that truly describes you, then you must first shift your mindset toward the long play for your organization. The long play is going to require teamwork.

What's included within the mindset shift to scaling social selling? First, you gather executive buy-in and make each role accountable for executing against a predefined set of key performance indicators (KPIs) that all align to one corporate goal.

What departments will be involved in a global social selling deployment?

- C-Level Commercial Leadership (Revenue Officer)

- VPs/Directors/Frontline Sales Managers
- All Sales Professionals from:
  - Demand/Lead Generation
  - Quota-Carrying Sales Closers
  - Customer Success/Account Management
  - Channel Partnerships
- Sales Operations and Sales Enablement
- Digital Content Marketing

Most Level 1 and Level 2 organizations that are executing some form of social selling are not thinking about all these departmental chess pieces. When I meet these organizations, they might be running pilot programs within inside sales or they might have a business unit or product group in one geographic region testing social selling. There is little to no inclusion for a joint task force of sales, marketing, sales operations, and enablement planning and executing together. The results are highly predictable as their social selling programs have minimal impact on revenue. Sure, they appear successful when they cite other KPIs such as increased engagement or more leads. But did their efforts really move the needle for the organization? The bigger challenge with this lack of departmental involvement is disruption. Certain business units are running a playbook that doesn't align with other business units' goals, especially when marketing isn't involved. You're, in essence, selling in a vacuum.

Collecting these stakeholders (e.g., sales leadership, marketing leadership, and operations/enablement leadership) might seem crazy as you first gather them into alignment. But it's absolutely the very first thing that Level 3, Social Selling Mastery, companies have done. These companies recognize that selling in a vacuum is ineffective and each department understands that working as one cohesive system will have a far greater impact on their respective business unit's success. Like a house of cards, remove one pillar, and the entire house falls to the ground.

CHAPTER 2

Leadership Executive Summary

Knowing is not enough, we must apply. Willing is not
enough, we must do.

—Bruce Lee

After you read this book, I hope you contact me to say, "This is the MBA of social selling." Each chapter provides you with the theory and principles up front, then dives deep into the tactics that need to be executed on a daily basis. This book is crafted in a sequence that should be followed in order of operations. Don't skip steps. Make Chapters 3, 4, and 5, the leadership chapters, a priority to execute, even if that takes months. We can't talk about Social Selling Mastery without first addressing the elephant in your organization—senior leaders. These executives *must* support, drive accountability, and reinforce social selling, to make it scale. This might seem like a blanket statement, but I can't be anymore straightforward. This is the first bridge you must cross. The leadership chapters will crack the code on the following:

1. Who needs to be part of your social selling project?
2. What are each leader's responsibilities and how does everyone contribute to driving accountability among all employees in the sales and digital marketing departments?
3. How do we measure social selling success from beginning to end, measuring and correlating the relationship between learning absorption and pipeline growth?
4. What will be our predictors for success and what should we be looking for as leading and current indicators in our sales and digital marketing teams?

After you have established a foundation for leadership to drive accountability, it's time to launch a program for both sales and marketing. While this book showcases the best practices for sales professionals first, training and developing marketing should happen simultaneously. Picture the sales and marketing departments learning at the same time and finding better ways to integrate as they're evolving. Your sales professionals will master a social selling routine that we call FEED, which stands for find, educate, engage, and develop. This will become their four-step dance routine to driving sales results at scale. The FEED system will ensure that sales professionals can answer the following social questions:

1. How do I create a social presence that resonates with my buyers?
2. What are the most effective ways to identify sales opportunities with social?
3. How do I start compelling conversations to open doors?
4. What is the most effective way to scale my social presence?
5. What should be my daily routine to maximize my return-on-effort?

In parallel, the digital marketing team is leveraging its own four-step dance routine, called CODE, which stands for create, organize, discover, and evaluate engagement. This process is designed specifically to fuel the sales team's social selling machine. Digital marketing will turn its department into a data-driven juggernaut that empirically measures its ability to fuel new clients (either directly or indirectly, through influence and attribution) and to help the sales team meet its quota. Marketing will have answers to the following:

1. How do we align our content production to fuel predictable sales results?
2. How do we create content at scale, with a purpose, that drives sales results?
3. What are the best practices for organizing content for the sales team to maximize its active engagement?
4. What are distribution tips and hacks to accelerate our exposure, and drive leads to sales with greater speed?
5. How do we measure trends and develop a roadmap to better improve our ability to fuel sales growth?

Finally, the glue between sales and marketing is the sales enablement team. This team will interweave social selling into the fabric of your sales process. Sales enablement and operations will bring together the right people, processes, and technology necessary to scale globally. Scale will be possible when enablement puts together a system to measure the effectiveness of the program from inception, to real-time deployment, to reinforcement actions, to return-on-investment.

As I mentioned before, this is your social selling MBA.

CHAPTER 3

How Do I Drive Organizational Buy-in and Accountability?

If you hang out with chickens, you're going to cluck and if your hang out with eagles, you're going to fly.
—Dr. Steve Maraboli

I'm going to start with a very bold statement. The success or failure of your Social Selling Mastery program, especially its becoming scalable, is predicated on senior leadership buy-in! All the other elements within the ecosystem of social selling are smaller in value to this one, very simple statement. I'd be lying if I pretended that turning it into reality was simple; unfortunately for some of you, this will be very complex.

I find it unfortunate that many senior leaders I meet don't share my passion for innovation within their commercial go-to-market strategy. In reality, I estimate that 80 percent of all senior leaders whom I meet before launching a social selling program are either skeptical, frustrated their routine will be altered, or downright scared. *Scared* is the right word, especially for senior marketers, because social selling puts the digital marketing team under the same microscope as a sales department. Marketers are just not used to having weekly, monthly, or quarterly meetings aimed at analyzing their production in which to turn their art into a science. Marketing isn't the only department from which you can anticipate pushback. The second potential red flag may come from your senior sales leaders, who many times view social selling as a widget, a thing, a pill that their sales professionals can take to magically hit quota. I often find sales leadership wants to get social selling training "over with" so the department can get back to "normal." What should worry you internally if you hear this is that "normal" is code for "this is an event; it will end, and we'll go back to the same way we've always done it." Sales leaders just want to hit quota, and plugging in a social selling widget sounds great if it means little disruption to normal. Finally, pay close attention to how sales enablement and sales operations show interest in social selling. I've found that, for traditional sales enablement leaders, their first natural instinct is to attack the problem with the same playbook they've always run:

1. Conduct a half-day, in-person workshop.
2. Find a tool that can do social selling.

With either of these solutions, you may hear the following statement: "Our sales professionals are already spread too thin and asked to do too much. They're constantly in meetings, and we can't take them out of the field for more training. Let's do a workshop when they're all together next month at QBR." If this is the path you choose, I can tell you with nearly 100 percent certainty that your organization will never digitally transform into a social-selling machine, especially a machine that significantly moves the sales needle. No half-day workshop or magical tool is going to drive millions of dollars into your sales pipeline. The root cause for these half-baked sales enablement solutions is a lack of commitment to true behavioral change. You can talk about change, but change is hard and takes time, and time is a luxury that most senior leaders feel they don't have. Again, I get it. According to Forrester, the average tenure of a senior sales leader is only 18 months![1]

---

[1] Forrester, September 6, 2014, https://salesbenchmarkindex.com/insights/sales
-leaders-try-something-dangerous/

If your window of opportunity is only 18 months, then make an innovative impact in your first six months! Give me six months to implement a Social Selling Mastery program with global scale, and I'll show you up to a 20 percent incremental sales uplift. But first, if you're a senior leader reading this book, it's time to grab a mirror and take a hard look at yourself. Are you going to be the change agent? Are you what the CEB would call a "Mobilizer"?[2] The road map to senior leadership driving change will be outlined next, but it's a moot point if you can't make changes to your own digital mindset. Where are social and digital strategies in your priorities?

PLOT YOUR SOCIAL SELLING MASTERY HIERARCHY OF NEEDS

Your Steps to a Successful Implementation

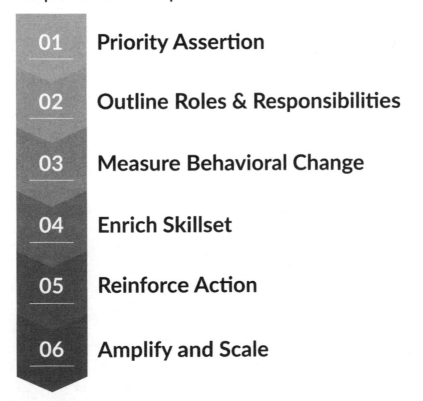

01	**Priority Assertion**
02	**Outline Roles & Responsibilities**
03	**Measure Behavioral Change**
04	**Enrich Skillset**
05	**Reinforce Action**
06	**Amplify and Scale**

---

[2] Corporate Executive Board (CEB), *The Challenger Customer*, https://www.cebglobal.com/top-insights/challenger-customer.html

I'm taking an idea from a simple system from my MBA coursework. At the time, Maslow's Hierarchy of Needs was perfect in helping me understand my personal need for survival to satisfaction, so I'll use this same formula to help you understand the Social Selling Mastery order of operations. This Social Selling Hierarchy of Needs is a linear process. To execute social selling at a global level, have your team follow the illustrated formula. You may have already had social pilots or small regional projects launched, but if you're going to go global, follow this process, which is discussed here and in the next two chapters.

PRIORITY ASSERTION

> *Action expresses priority.*
>
> —Mahatma Gandhi

Your company has thousands of ideas and projects in motion. Within the sales department, some new initiatives will be product-based and others will be skill-based. Through experience, I'm a firm believer that social selling scaled throughout an organization is only possible when it's a top-three sales initiative globally. Otherwise, the pilot execution is only a nice-to-have mindshare. Social selling is not like launching a product, but unfortunately, average sales enablement teams deploy it as though it were. Products require a sales professional's brain to be filled with features, advantages, and benefits so he or she can be competent in a buyer conversation. Social selling is a principle and process in which each sales professional plays a part of a sequence. This sequence doesn't end! This sequence isn't crammed into a sales professional's head once and turned on like a light switch. Because it's an *initiative*, senior leaders need to be committed to the notion that social and digital interactions are the way we're going to compliment working with buyers going forward. It's **infinite** and will have a priority level that doesn't turn off next quarter.

To help establish social selling as a priority, successful implementations start with building a communications plan. Priorities need to be articulated. Priorities need to be continuously addressed to all participating departments, multiple times, for the message to resonate. Every time I address building a communications plan with senior executives, I love to use the old analogy of bringing a horse to water, but not being able to make it drink. This timeless analogy is a metaphor to explain the most important part of your communications plan; you must drink the water first, and then your team will follow. No matter the sequence, frequency, and method of communicating your plan (e.g., town hall meetings, sales kick-offs, quarterly business reviews, video emails, etc.), your actions will far outweigh any communicated presentation. Of course, social selling has the best chance of excelling if expressed as a top priority, with enthusiasm, from the highest C-level executives. As an example, in small and medium-sized businesses (SMBs), where the CEO is actively involved with the sales force, he or she needs to be the voice for digital transformation. After expressing social selling as a priority, C-level executives can use some of these simple actions to demonstrate their sincerity:

1. Tweet company successes.
2. Connect with the entire sales and marketing team on LinkedIn.
3. Share favorite digital articles and insights with the salesforce as recommended reading and sharing.
4. Be part of digital asset creation through blog articles or videos.

These subtle but highly impactful actions will speak volumes to the sales and marketing teams, who will immediately see a newly developed importance for embracing the digital world.

CHAPTER 4

The Three Key Leadership Roles

Sales, Marketing, and Sales Operations/Enablement

Get the right people on the bus, the wrong people off the bus, and the right people in the right seats.
—Jim Collins

OUTLINE ROLES AND RESPONSIBILITIES

We call your core social selling committee "the three amigos." The three amigos are made up of three senior leadership types:

1. Sales Leader(s)
2. Marketing Leader(s)
3. Operations/Enablement Leader(s)

The organization must mandate that all three divisional leaders are equally part of social selling planning and execution. Each role will be a vital dance partner. Don't discount any role's involvement in success or you'll risk everything falling apart. If you're part of a small or medium-size business (SMB) in which one of these roles doesn't exist, that's completely fine. The important part is understanding what these three job functions require for overall social selling success. Using this information, you can plot a course to share these responsibilities with others in your organization.

1. Sales Leader(s)

You are the voice of accountability. We've seen marketers, sales operations, and/or sales enablement leaders champion a social selling program by themselves. The result has nearly been a 100-percent failure rate because the sales professional ultimately does not report to those roles. With proper sales leadership accountability, a sales professional will learn a new skill and the sales leader will be responsible for helping to ensure that newly acquired skill is actioned into a sales outcome. Sales leadership, more than the other amigos' roles, is a lead-by-example role. Using our leading a horse-to-water analogy, the person in this role must be prepared to drink the water first. Remember, sales professionals want to be you! They look up to their sales VPs. Sales professionals will emulate you because they assume your actions are a reflection of what made you so successful. Don't forget that you as a sales leader are under the microscope of tens, hundreds, or thousands of sales professionals each day. If you're social, they'll become social. I can't make it simpler than that!

The second way to drive accountability is to manage and coach social selling in your one-on-ones. In his book *Sales Management. Simplified*, Mike Weinberg talks extensively about the importance of the one-on-one between sales professionals and their sales leader. The results of successful one-on-one coaching are straightforward: You get the results that you measure and coach toward. If you don't explore your sales team's social activity as part of your one-on-ones, how can you expect it to happen? If you're constantly reinforcing elements of social selling to go deeper and wider into accounts, expect that social will become part of their daily cadence. Here is a tactical example of what you can implement:

1. Before your sales professionals learn a new social selling action, you learn the action first.
2. You then contextualize the action for the sales team (why it's important, how it works within your sales process, what value it will provide).
3. Later, reinforce that same social selling action at each one-on-one meeting until you feel each sales professional has incorporated this action into his or her sales DNA.
4. Once the previous action has become habitual, layer on a new social selling action into a sales professional's daily cadence.

2. Marketing Leader(s)

You are the engine that powers the social selling machine. You are so critical, but often overlooked in a social selling implementation. I'm going to call out companies now: If you think your organization has a handle on social selling, but Part 3 of this book is not part of your go-to-market strategy, you're not a social selling organization! Here's the rub: What will be expected of you and your team from a digital content marketing perspective is most likely far beyond what you're implementing today. Don't panic. You've bought this book to understand the road map. You will be expected to run a data-driven machine, and this will most likely entail throwing away the current ways of measuring your progress. A social selling organization has its marketing team measured against its delivered percentage contribution of sales quota attainment. **That's it!** And you're most likely nowhere near this today. This simple accountability change is where you'll establish your first mindset shift. Gone are the days of thinking about website traffic, clicks, opens, retweets, and lead volume. None of these metrics are going to be sufficient goals for your team in 2016 and beyond. As we explore marketing's role in greater detail, you'll notice the importance of getting back to the fundamentals. One such example will be co-developing a buyer's journey with the sales department. This future alignment between sales and marketing will allow for much faster and more effective insight creation, which will fuel buyer conversations. Marketing must become the factory that creates and organizes this content to help expand the discovery of these digital insights by your buyers. Marketing must also develop ways to measure this engagement. Your analysis will go deeper than you've ever gone before by measuring the complete *content-consumption story* of every buyer in your funnel. The trends you'll discover will help create a prescriptive road map to both improving your production throughput and increasing lead conversion for your sales team. You're ultimately responsible for helping a sales professional create value *first*, before your competition, which according to Forrester, establishes the sales professional to win 74 percent of those deals.[1]

3. Sales Operations/Enablement Leader(s)

Sales operations and sales enablement is the glue between sales and marketing. Your responsibility is to bring all the people, processes, and technology together into one workable system. We have found that successful social selling implementations come from progressive enablement teams that have no fear pushing the internal sales status quo. These progressive leaders have no time or patience for sales professionals who complain about not having time for training. These enablement leaders know that learning behavior is a leading indicator to future sales success.

One of your first steps is visualizing the current sales process in complete transparency, taking into account roles of both sales and marketing. After plotting your sales process, gain approval from the sales and marketing departments so you have their agreement that this is your go-to-market system. After that, you can interweave where

---

[1] Forrester, January 27, 2014, http://blogs.forrester.com/mark_lindwall/14-01 -27-to_win_against_increasing_competition_equip_your_salespeople_with_a_ deeper_understanding_of_your_buy

social selling slots into that process. Eighty-five percent of your sales and marketing teammates are visual learners[2]—so leverage visual documents that help everyone see the tactical steps. This visualization is the basis for an accountability document you'll create called the service-level agreement. Social selling is an additive process that complements your existing sales process. *Do not* attempt to boil the ocean by trying to reengineer a huge portion of your sales process for social selling in one dramatic fashion. All you're going to get from sales professionals are blank stares and rolling eyes. Your goal is to showcase tactical steps that sales professionals have been missing. With a slight altering to their current activity within their current process, they would be effectively social selling.

---

[2] Hubspot, August 6, 2012. Blog, http://blog.hubspot.com/blog/tabid/6307/bid/33423/19-Reasons-You-Should-Include-Visual-Content-in-Your-Marketing -Data.aspx

CHAPTER 5

Organizational Tools and Metrics for Social Selling Success

True education flowers at the point when delight falls in love with responsibility.

—Philip Pullman

MEASURE BEHAVIORAL CHANGE

Sales operations (and marketing operations, if your company has them) are the lynchpin to developing your social selling key performance indicator (KPI) metrics and milestones, and aligning these to corporate goals. You will centralize the numbers to create one source of truth. I cannot stress enough that improper metrics is where social selling programs crash and burn the fastest. If you don't have the appropriate KPIs in place, any hopes of a global rollout have been stifled even before the pilot has begun. The reason for this failure is that, without proper centralized metrics in place, the three amigos department leaders begin creating their own metrics in a vacuum, based on what each considers important. In even worse cases, I've seen many departmental leaders decide to roll out a social selling program, without ever informing the other departments that the program even exists. How can you have expected to succeed without a unified program? Your goals may have little consequence to the overall corporate goals and initiatives. Ultimately, and I've watched this misalignment unravel against my constant advice, the failed program ends in a company blame game.

1. If sales leadership is not aligned, there will be little accountability for sales professionals to drive social selling actions with any consistency.
2. If marketing is left in the dark, then the sales force will be without sufficient content and inbound leads to fuel buyer conversations.
3. If enablement hasn't made designing a continued education plan part of the package, then expect the sales force to revert to old habits in short order.

To mitigate this frustration up front, get sales, marketing, and sales operations or sales enablement leaders in a room and develop answers to the question, "What does success look like for you?" Remember, people are typically self-serving, so get their needs out on the table. Listen to what success means for each of these departments and begin crafting a common goal. What shared successes can you all align to? From this vision, begin creating more tactical goals for each department. Each goal has to be quantifiable—no fluff, no subjection.

Here is an example of that alignment:

What does success look like for the company?
  The CEO said on our last conference call that, within six months, we need to create a 20 percent incremental uplift in the sales pipeline. That sales pipeline growth can come from either new prospective accounts or existing accounts.

What does success look like for sales leadership?
  Of the 20 percent sales corporate goal, the sales force will contribute 50 percent. That equals 10 percent, half of the 20 percent

incremental uplift required. This half from sales will be a socially driven pipeline from direct sales activity.

What does success look like for marketing leadership?

Of the 20 percent sales corporate goal, digital marketing will contribute 50 percent. That equals 10 percent, half of the 20 percent incremental uplift required. The half from marketing will be from inbound leads driven by digital insights. The other 50 percent (which sales is being measured against) will be marketing's responsibility to map the indirect lead Attribution (within the content consumption story) of each buyer in the pipeline, showing the value insights are having on sales pipeline.

What does success look like for sales enablement?

To make this sales pipeline growth possible, within the first 90 days, 90 percent of the sales team will be certified on social selling through a written and practical test. The certification will be a combination of a multiple-choice exam, plus practicum presentation. The practicum will have each sales professional create a new lead using social selling activity and present that new lead to their sales manager for verification. By multiplying one new lead per sales professional, we will reach the sales pipeline goals necessary for the required sales-portion of our social selling KPIs.

> *Repetition is the mother of all learning.*
>
> —Zig Ziglar

LEADING –> CURRENT –> LAGGING INDICATORS FOR SUCCESS

I often mention the above quote from Zig Ziglar because he was dead right; behavioral change happens through practice. Not only is practice so critical to your development, but it's also the only way I see behavioral changes sticking at a scalable level within your company. Often, I'll meet commercial leaders who, by no fault of their own, immediately want to measure only how much money the organization made from social sales. Don't get me wrong, this is *the most important* measure, but sales from social selling is a lagging indicator of success. Remember growth is a marathon, not a 100-meter dash. Measuring socially driven sales will give you a snapshot of the last 90 or 180 days, but what can you do if you're not hitting your quota? You can't do a darn thing right now to change that shortcoming! That correction should have been made weeks or months ago. My advice is to change your mindset to think about measuring three levels of indicators: leading, current, and lagging.

Leading Indicators

What KPIs can we look at to ensure we're moving in the right direction? I'm a huge believer that learning, and the willingness to learn, is a leading indicator. Let's use the analogy of high school students. A teacher has a goal that 100 percent of her students be accepted into a college or university at the end of the school year. Acceptance into postsecondary education is her lagging indicator. If the teacher has only 90 percent of the students accepted, there is nothing she can do about it at the end of the school year. She would have needed to look at key behavioral triggers and homework activity (leading and current indicators) that could have helped her make prescriptive changes to specific students' outcomes. Continuing this analogy, a teacher may use a student's in-class participation as a leading indicator. Students who sit in the front of the classroom and answer in-class questions typically show a higher propensity to have learned the curriculum. Returning to your social selling program, how is your sales enablement team looking for triggers to determine a leading indicator? Are your sales and marketing professionals attending your training and are they attentive? Are they doing the required assignments? Just like high school, the students who pay attention to the teacher and curriculum have a higher probability of successfully acing their upcoming pop quizzes (a traditional current indicator used in high school).

Current Indicators

In high school, a teacher uses pop quizzes to determine if a student is comprehending the curriculum and can translate these new learnings into application. Your sales force is no different. You have tools that measure if new learnings are being translated into sales outcomes. Examples of these tools are:

- **Customer relationship management (CRM):** Are your sales professionals having new social conversations logged as activity?
- **Marketing automation:** Are new leads being driven through social campaigns? What effect is social having on the number of new leads?
- **LinkedIn Sales Navigator:** Are your sales professionals leveraging the tool on a daily basis? Which teammates are consistent users and driving new social conversations?
- **Employee Advocacy:** Are your sales professionals consistently sharing insights? How are your sales team's social networks becoming lead generation machines for your company?

Whether you're a sales, marketing, or sales operations/enablement leader, you can leverage social selling current indicators to gather a snapshot of your team's success. The value of current indicators is that they provide real-time information to help you make prescriptive course corrections. Are certain sales or marketing professionals falling behind? Do most of these failing professionals report to a specific leader? Perhaps this leader hasn't been holding staff accountable for social activity? There are multiple tools you can leverage to monitor current sales outcomes. We explore setting up these tools in greater detail later in this chapter. Warning: Don't get hung up on measurables and KPIs; that can derail your efforts to start a social selling program. I know you want to measure success, but what is the opportunity cost of not engaging your customers in this digital world? I've seen hundreds of companies delay making any changes internally (social or otherwise) because their CRM and marketing automation systems were a mess. These companies have data paralysis. For all the time, money, and resources needed to fix their data problem, they're losing millions of dollars a month to competitors who are building digital relationships with their customers. Don't let data paralysis be your Achilles' heel. Get into the market!

Lagging Indicators

Back to our high school analogy, those students who sat in the front of the classroom, raising their hands for every question, typically aced their pop quizzes and achieved the teacher's ultimate lagging indicator goal—acceptance to the best college and universities. If a teacher hadn't created a mechanism to measure progression throughout the course of the school year, she could have been massively disappointed when a group of students failed the final exam—especially if there had been something she could have done to change some of those outcomes. Your sales and marketing teams are no different. You're going to kick yourself if you spend time, money, and energy, only to find out that 20 percent of your sales force is executing socially, while the rest of the sales team has reverted to status quo. Your CRM and marketing automation platforms aren't going to change behavior. I believe that only proper coaching and training can alter the trajectory of proper digital transformations inside an organization.

To help you build a foundation for measuring success, here is a tactical road map to follow when setting up your indicators.

SETTING UP YOUR LEADING INDICATORS

If you can't measure it, you can't control it.
—John Grebe

The big difference I find between social media for sales and social selling is the latter's up-front approach to measurement. I often find that companies that have developed their own "Social Selling 101" courses put little thought into measuring baselines and setting goals for incremental improvements. You and your organization won't make these mistakes because you intend to scale social selling at a global level with tremendous success. First of all, you must work in tandem with your sales operations/enablement team. In fact, I'm going to talk through this process as though I'm speaking to the sales operations/ enablement leader.

You're a professional coach and/or trainer who recognizes the importance that people, process, and technology, working in harmony, have on your sales force. You naturally think about ways to measure the effectiveness of your sales performance initiatives. This is perfect because these measurements will be your leading indicators for understanding how training a new skill has soaked into your sales team's DNA. For many mid-market and enterprise organizations, you have an internal learning portal, often referred to as a learning management system (LMS). If you have an LMS, great, but if you don't, don't fret. The core value of an LMS is to help measure the learning behavior of your team. Any tool can house your training curriculum. True value comes when that tool can help you segment your team into categories such as laggards, core performers, and rock stars. Regardless of whether you have an LMS, you need to find a process to answer these questions:

- What students are regular attendees and absentees from your training sessions?
- What students are showing engagement and excitement for applying their new skills?
- What students are continuing their learning (via video, workbooks, guides, discussions, etc.) beyond the initial training sessions?

Like the high school teacher in our analogy, you're segmenting your classroom. Who do you need to focus your attention on and which students seem to be natural learners? It doesn't take very long to determine who your most engaged students are and I recommend focusing on them to shine a spotlight on their successes. This is critical if you're in the early stages of a pilot group that is testing social selling. You'll focus on these engaged students because you want to showcase their achievements and, ultimately, correlate their actions to sales.

Taking leading indicators to another level, some clients of ours will work with us to audit and assess their team in advance of training. They'll make a traditional list of top-performing sales professionals (as a percentage of sales against their own sales quota) flowing downward to the least effective. We'll then tag *potential social sellers* based on historical sales success. This helps prove a potential theory that successful sales professionals are both the most open to learning new skills and the most likely to apply these new skills. Without diving deep into assessing your organization's learning culture, you can start seeking to prove a few hypotheses you may have:

- Will all the social sellers be your only high performers or do you have core performers and laggards eager to improve?
- Over time, how did social selling help a sales professional either progress or fall along the stack-rank list?
- Using all your leading indicator data, do you better understand your new-hire strategy? Should you be looking for specific signals from applicants that can help predict if they'll embrace social selling?

Here is what I anticipate you'll see within your initial training rollout. Twenty percent of your sales team is already high performing. Of those 20 percent, 50 percent will already be socially engaged (a great sign, helping your business case), while the other 50 percent will digest one to two new skills. It will be more difficult to convince this second half of high performers to change their core sales cadence. Your core performers will account for between 50 and 70 percent of your team. You're going to find most of these core performers are eager to learn new skills. If they believe in your program, they will follow it as designed. Remember, a core performer is only a few opportunities and deals away from hitting quota. Core performers typically know that a few changes to their sales cadence can make up this difference. According to the CEB, a 5 percent incremental improvement by your core performers can have up to a 60 percent increase in sales for your business.[1]

The challenge is that the party doesn't end after the skill-based training. If you want your core performers to permanently improve their sales behavior, design education touchpoints (e.g., extra help sessions, one-on-one mentoring, etc.) to sustain continuous practice. These core performers aren't the rock stars, who already may have social selling in their DNA. If you're having trouble engaging specific core performers, leverage stories from their peers to show how specific tactical examples are having an impact. Core performers are still highly competitive and, generally, open to learning new skills that will translate into hitting their sales quotas.

Finally, we come to your laggards, the bottom 10 to 20 percent of sales performers who are going to be detractors, skeptical and disengaged. As this book is about scale, my personal opinion is that you should focus little attention on the laggards. The return-on-effort (ROE) will be minimal, as a small improvement in low sales-quota attainment brings only slightly less disappointing results. After working with 60,000 sales and marketing professionals, I can tell you that laggards have one foot out the door, either because of your dissatisfaction or of their own volition. Of course, offer them training, but don't spin your wheels trying to ensure that they adopt social selling. Not every sales professional on your staff will come aboard, so set realistic expectations.

Why are leading indicators critical?

Let me provide a customer example that empirically proves that learning behavior has a direct impact on your sales pipeline. Our customer, CA Technologies, has done an excellent job of this. After deploying Social Selling Mastery globally to thousands of sales professionals, their story is as follows.

If a sales professional finished the training program, on average, they created 15 percent more revenue and had a 12 percent larger sales pipeline than their peers who completed only 70 percent of the

---

[1] CEB, July 26, 2010, https://www.cebglobal.com/blogs/six-myths-of-sales -performance/

training. Compared to their peers who completed only 40 percent of the training, the certified team created 36 percent more revenue and had a 28 percent larger sales pipeline. If they weren't keeping a close eye on students progressing through the program to course correct them on the way to certification, CA Technologies could miss out on 15 to 36 percent more revenue. At scale, that's millions and millions of dollars.

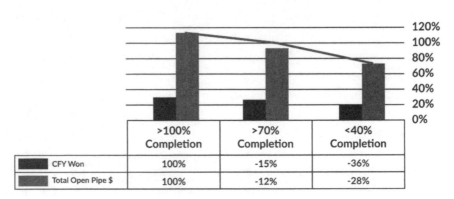

Social Selling Completion

	>100% Completion	>70% Completion	<40% Completion
CFY Won	100%	-15%	-36%
Total Open Pipe $	100%	-12%	-28%

Your leading indicators don't end at measuring learning behavior. This is a perfect opportunity to measure your sales team's previous social activity as a signal for potential social selling success. Using current indicators (later in this chapter), you'll want to understand if these new skills are changing behavior or if the training has only reinforced actions that the sales team is already executing. Capture baselines that you intend to use to show behavioral change or skill improvement based on your training and coaching. To help you start thinking at a tactical level, here are questions you'll want to pose to your sales and marketing teams in advance of a social selling program.

Sales

- What percentage of your accounts do you track online to provide you automatic, digitally emailed triggers?

- Within your accounts, and among the main contacts who work there, what percentage have you connected to on LinkedIn, Twitter, or Facebook?
- What size were your social networks before starting any training program?
- In the last week, how often did you share digital insights with any of your buyers?

Marketing

- What is your team's direct contribution to the sales team's quota attainment? Do you know the exact sales bookings that flowed through your inbound marketing system to the sales team?
- What is your current content production schedule, by volume and velocity (i.e., the speed it takes to create one new content unit), separated by different asset types such as blogs versus ebooks?
- What are the best performing insights when it comes to traffic engagement and lead conversion?
- What percentage of the sales team is leveraging your digital insights, either through your content library or employee advocacy tool?

The answers to these questions are your baselines.

SET UP YOUR CURRENT INDICATORS

The simplest way to think about your current indicators is: Look at a teammate right now and determine if today he or she is turning a previously learned skill into a defined action. To measure this you need to leverage tools to capture real-time information. Here are the most commonly leveraged tools for capturing and presenting real-time current indicators:

- CRM
- Marketing automation
- Your sales team's social platforms, such as LinkedIn
- Content engagement (such as employee advocacy)

In high school, your teachers leveraged a variety of current indicators to help them gauge alignment to their goal. Your teachers asked you to create book reports and speeches, engage in spelling bees and debates, and of course take tests, all in an effort to measure real-time outcomes.

To properly set up your current indicators, you'll need to imagine the mindset of your buyer. Start with a buyer's journey and think about how he or she first engages with your company. CEB found that "57% of that journey is happening before the sales team has made initial contact,"[2] meaning that your buyer is leveraging digital content much earlier than you anticipate, and thus this data needs to be measured. This is where your marketing automation platform provides tremendously contextual information about your buyers' content consumption story. Marketing automation is going to help your organization understand how leads originate and how buyers interact with your business throughout their entire buying journey. Within your marketing automation platform, you'll want to benchmark the following questions, then measure the incremental improvements on these actions:

- How are you creating new leads leveraging social media today? What social platforms do you use? What campaigns have been especially effective?
- Are there specific digital insights that are triggering new leads better than others?
- Do you know whether specific sales professionals are driving these new leads via their social activity?

These are examples of questions that any marketing automation platform can answer. By creating a baseline for these questions, your

---

[2] CEB, March 31, 2015, https://www.cebglobal.com/blogs/b2b-sales-and-marketing-two-numbers-you-should-care-about/

team can plot a course to make improvements on a weekly, monthly, or quarterly basis. Tactical examples of this could be:

- Ninety days ago, we created 13 percent of our new leads socially. Today, we've improved to 17 percent. Nearly all these leads are driven via LinkedIn.
- Eighty-five percent of these new leads came from our last three webinars. The other 15 percent came from our ebook "X Triggers to Improving Y."
- Sam, Daniel, and Charlene from the sales team are driving the majority of new leads from their LinkedIn profiles, thus these new leads are not just originating from our corporate LinkedIn network. Our sales professionals are becoming real lead generation engines!

Employee advocacy tools are distribution and engagement amplifiers to digital insights, which increase in value if you're properly tracking this engagement in your marketing automation. Employee advocacy tools also have their own tracking mechanisms, which many times showcase usage, content sharing volume, basic click engagement, and stack ranks for your sales team. Employee advocacy can provide excellent current indicator data for content engagement, which is a critical part of social selling. But *do not* substitute employee advocacy metrics for CRM and marketing automation data, otherwise you'll be missing major drivers.

By far, the most important tool for measuring current indicators in real time is your CRM—hands down! Sales and marketing leaders had traditionally been apprehensive about implementing social selling because they didn't know how to measure it. This is odd because this is precisely what makes social selling amazing. Social selling is made up of digital activity, all of which can be logged in your CRM. The capturing of activities for reports and dashboards needs to follow the same logical sequence as your buyer traveling throughout his or her buying journey:

- How are leads being created? Are the leads flowing from marketing or has the sales department developed its own leads from social activity?

- How are sales professionals approaching their buyer (e.g., phone, email, social)? Are they leveraging digital insights as part of these conversations? How do you log that activity?
- What leads are converting to opportunities? Is social selling having a direct contribution or indirect influence on new opportunities?

All of these questions can be answered within CRM fields for leads, activities, accounts, and opportunities. For most organizations, this simply requires adding new tabs for social or LinkedIn within their existing picklists. Measuring social selling in your CRM should not be transformational, only additive. If you're measuring emails and phone calls, you can measure social activity.

The final tools that help you measure current indicators are the sales team's social platforms. Map the activities within LinkedIn or Twitter that can demonstrate that sales professionals' newly learned skills are translating into positive sales actions. Examples of these measures are:

- What percentage of a sales professional's assigned accounts and contacts (from your CRM) are now being followed by that sales professional on Twitter and LinkedIn? Has the sales professional connected to all the decision makers, champions, or influencers in that account on LinkedIn?
- Is the sales professional consistently sharing digital insights to his or her entire social network? How often?
- Is the sales professional consistently growing his or her social reach? What is the rate of growth in relationship to his or her sales territory opportunity?

LINKEDIN SALES NAVIGATOR AS A CURRENT INDICATOR

LinkedIn Sales Navigator helps your organization mechanize the LinkedIn platform for current-indicator measurement. I've found the platform evolves beyond general prospecting and becomes an excellent account-centric sales tool. Its ultimate value is LinkedIn speed-to-execution and, depending on the size of your organization, the scaling speed can mean huge man-hour savings. LinkedIn Sales Navigator arrogates many of your sales team's natural processes with a regular LinkedIn account but it packages the process for account-based selling. Save 10 minutes per day for 250 business days, times 1,000 sales professionals, and the speed-to-execution becomes massively important. As you're seeking ways to leverage the tool for measurement, LinkedIn's Social Selling Index Score (SSI Score) is an obvious choice. This is a combination of four key factors that make up ideal social selling behavior—*building a personal brand, finding the right buyers, engaging with insights, and building strong relationships.* This score out of 100 is a gauge for your team to stack rank team members and compare their performance against that of industry peers. You can also leverage the reporting section to give you highly valuable information on the following:

- What is our usage and adoption?
- Are we socially surrounding our accounts?
- Are we committing to social engagement?

On a daily basis, you want your sales team to find social signals and create greater conversational engagement. LinkedIn Sales Navigator will centralize that information.

SET UP YOUR LAGGING INDICATORS

Lagging indicators are the sales pipeline and sales bookings results that appear on your CRM dashboards. You now are seeing what social selling activity over the past 90, 180, and 365 days has yielded for your sales and marketing organization. I highly recommend you create one version of the truth by creating a central social selling dashboard in your CRM. This dashboard will show the leads, social activity, opportunities, and sales bookings attributed to social selling.

I believe the most overlooked lagging indicator is the content consumption story that your buyers are providing. This is the road map of digital fingerprints your buyers are leaving throughout your business on their journey to become a customer. While we set up your marketing automation platform to track digital insights consumed and lead sourcing, the real value from marketing will come from trend analysis on your buyers. Over time, you will know how your buyer buys, what they read and watch, and when, how often, and in what context to specific interactions with your sales force. This data will transform how your sales team approaches all future buyers with digital insights. Sales team members will have a much better appreciation and understanding of how best to help a buyer along their learning path. We'll be diving deep into the content consumption story in Part Three, "Building a lead factory with digital content marketing." For now, remember that social selling can be tracked throughout your buyer's entire journey—those journeys can be evaluated for trends and prescriptive improvements.

SOCIAL SELLING MASTERY FOR THE SALES PROFESSIONAL

Start Building a Personal Brand

If people like you, they will listen to you, but if they trust you, they'll do business with you.

—Zig Ziglar

ENRICH SKILLSET

In a survey of 300 sales professionals conducted by Feedback Systems, Sales for Life, PeopleLinx, Sandler Training, Sales Readiness Group, and VorsightBP, 72 percent of sales professionals do not feel they have a proficient social selling process.[1] If you feel this is you, it's because you've never been given a clear, prescriptive process to follow. My job is to provide that clarity and distill the noise into focus.

---

[1] Sales for Life, December 9, 2015, http://www.salesforlife.com/resources#ufh-i -211476051-the-state-of-social-selling-in-2016-infographic/185466

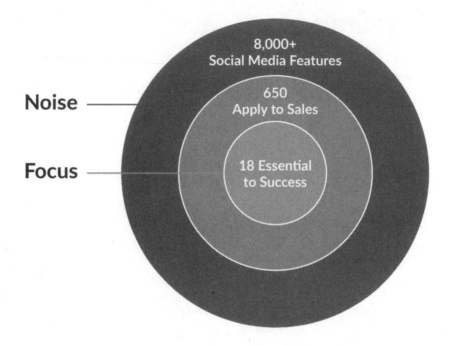

Don't be distracted by social media features, even if people have suggested that a particular one can apply to sales. I'm going to show you the routine that more than 60,000 sales professionals are leveraging each day to:

- Open new doors more quickly and frequently.
- Nurture their accounts to increase the velocity and probability that they win the deal.
- Become the voice for your industry, helping you create residual opportunities you haven't seen before.

To accomplish these goals, you will be learning a four-step system that will simplify your social selling strategy. The following four steps are to leverage every deal.

Develop   **Find**

Engage   **Educate**

1. **Find** a buyer, his or her buying committee, and his or her buying influences, then socially surround all these people to gather market intelligence.
2. **Educate** yourself and your buyer to have more contextual conversations that build rapport and trust. Digital insights are key to shaping a buyer's journey.
3. **Engage** your buyers with digital insights that push them off their status quo so they think differently about their go-to-market priorities.
4. **Develop** a network of people that can continue to open opportunities for you. You recognize that your "network is your net worth," to borrow a phrase from Jill Rowley.[2]

THIS JOURNEY BEGINS WITH A NEW MINDSET

Clear your mind and erase your perspective of social media, specifically LinkedIn. Unfortunately, for so many sales professionals, our online and offline social networks have been a closed circuit of personal relationships. Few of us have extended our networks far beyond our friends, employer, job function, or city. From an online prospective, the reason I believe this issue exists is because of the rise of Facebook before LinkedIn and other social platforms. For millions of people, Facebook was their introduction to social networking; heck,

---

[2] Hubspot, April 3, 2014, http://blog.hubspot.com/sales/social-selling-jill-rowley

even my grandmother is on Facebook. If you look at your Facebook friends, I would venture to guess that you have between 150 to 300 friends. Most of these friends are either in your current inner-circle of friends today or from your past (e.g., high school and college friends). On Facebook, you are sharing intimate photos and stories about your personal life, for which these posts are directed to people whom you know quite well. Since this was your first impression of social networking, you carried over that same philosophy to LinkedIn and Twitter. On average, most sales professionals globally have fewer than 500 first-degree connections on LinkedIn and, with the exception of a few work colleagues and business connections, their Facebook and LinkedIn networks look basically the same.

Do you see the problem with that?

I'll paint the problem in an analogy I love to use. Suppose you were invited to a massive networking event, and by *massive*, I mean the world's largest. This major event symbolizes the more than 420 million people networking on LinkedIn at the time of this publication. After you received the invite to this networking event, you have been given two options: (1) to sit at home on your couch and not attend the event, missing this perfect networking opportunity, or (2) join the event, grab a drink, and start networking. Clearly, option 2 places you in a far greater position to create opportunities. Yet, it's remarkable how few sales professionals have seen social media as a means of quickly connecting with buyers at speeds that were impossible until only a few years ago. While many people talk about social selling as a brand-building or networking opportunity, I like to distill it to the most important element to any sales professional: *speed-to-revenue*.

What I'd like you to do is think of your LinkedIn and Twitter profiles as digital newspapers. How do newspapers generate revenue? They attract more and more subscribers! You're going to start seeing your own social connections as subscribers, and the more prospective buyers who are part of your subscription base, the more you'll be able to influence and shape their buying decisions. Let's now rename these subscribers as *advocates*. The more advocates you add to your network, the more you become a digital new resource for them. This means these advocates can have a stronger positive impact on your business. As you attract advocates, there are three core benefits they will provide yover a period of time:

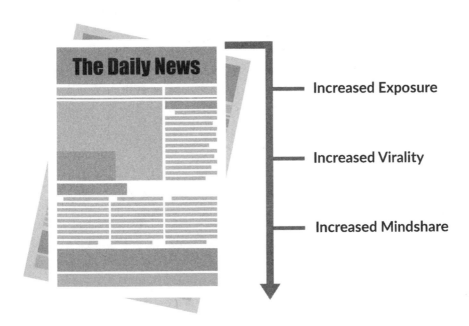

1. Increased exposure probability.

Throughout this book, you learn how to share digital insights to educate, inform, and provide value to your buyer. For typical sales professionals, ideal buyers are sitting outside their networks as second-degree connections on LinkedIn and non-followers on Twitter. That means that as you share insights, the only way your ideal buyer would see your insights is if someone in your mutual first-degree connections liked, commented on, or shared the insights, and they push these insights to your buyer through their connections. But, if you become a first-degree connection on LinkedIn, or this buyer Follows you on Twitter, each time you share insights, he or she gains direct access to your information. Just like a great television commercial, the more a brand is placed in front of people, the more it begins to influence them. You need more exposure!

2. Increased viral probability.

In March 2011, I had approximately 500 LinkedIn first-degree connections and a few hundred Twitter followers. My *social reach* was terrible. As a reminder, social reach is the percentage of your target market (prospective buyers, clients, industry thought-leaders) that makes up your entire social network. If you have 500 first-degree LinkedIn connections, yet only 50 people make up your current target market, then you have a 10 percent social reach. Depending on your sales role, 50 people could be strong (if you're working a few strategic accounts) or poor if you've been assigned a territory with thousands of accounts.

Back in March 2011, my social reach wasn't strong enough to help me accomplish my goals and that really became apparent when I shared insights on LinkedIn. As I would share insights about sales best practices, only a fraction of the people in my LinkedIn network would find my insights of value. As you're now thinking about your own social presence, the more people you connect with who are prospective buyers, clients, and industry experts, the more people you can continue to influence. The more insights that you share, and the more insights these people are exposed to, the more these people will be inspired to share your insights with their network. Now, you're about to experience a multiplier effect. Your insights are not only seen by your network, but also by second-degree connections you've never met! These second-degree connections will have similar job functions to the first-degree connections you've been sharing insights with, thus exposing you to more opportunities.

3. Increased mindshare probability.

This may sound obvious, but the more exposure a buyer has to you over time, the more crystalized their vision of your value becomes. Trust me, it's far better to be there too often than to be forgotten. Think of the local real estate agent in your neighborhood who has 15 billboards, fridge magnets, park bench signs, and a never-ending list of open houses on Sundays. Now, unless one of your great friends is a real estate agent, your natural instinct is to gravitate to this super-marketer realtor who appears to be the most trusted and knowledgeable, and the most likely to yield the best ROI on your home. That super-marketing realtor will definitely be on the top of your mind come house-selling time. While this is a business-to-consumer analogy, guess what? *People are people.* People are inspired and influenced by advertisements for home real estate the same way they are influenced by insights for enterprise resource planning (ERP) software, financial services, or medical devices. Become top of mind or I promise you that your competitors will be! I can't stress this enough for your future self:

> *Obscurity is a bigger problem than money.*
> —Grant Cardone

Get into this social market!

CHAPTER 7

Develop Buyer-Centric Profiles

LinkedIn, Twitter, and Other Social Platforms

You will never get a second chance to make a first impression.

—Will Rogers

The critical phrase in this chapter is buyer-centric. Who is your buyer? I'm certain your buyer is not a recruiter. Then why, when I read your LinkedIn profile, does it resonate with a recruiter? Stop to think about what your first impression is leaving:

1. Quota-crusher
2. Sales negotiation expert
3. President's Club winner, three years in a row

You buyer doesn't care about that! None of these statements do anything to aid the challenges your buyer is facing in their business.

Everything you do socially needs to better serve your buyer. Period. I fully appreciate that you may not work at your current employer forever, but what message are you sending your future employer? To me, the message sounds like: "I don't use social media in my current job and I'm most likely not going to leverage it at your company either, as I'm keeping my options open." The very first step to developing an ideal social profile on any platform is taking a moment to accomplish two steps.

Step 1: Take an objective look in the mirror.
Open your social profiles and read them aloud. Read your profiles as if you were a buying CFO, CIO, and so on, and ask yourself, "What's in it for me?" Do your buyers feel comfortable that you understand their business? Are you sending the message that you can add value in their business?

Step 2: Take an objective look at your buyers' profiles.
Your buyers are leaving clues about their industry all over their own social profiles: keywords, phrases, trends, ways they measure and benchmark themselves. This information can be found on LinkedIn in their summary, their skills, and the groups they join. Within Twitter, I find that the photos they take can be a huge gateway into their world. I'm looking at the conferences they attend and the inspirational quotes they share. All of these elements help me think about crafting my social profile to mirror my buyer's. People buy from people they like, and people like people just like themselves.

LINKEDIN PHOTO SHOWCASES TRUST

Ask yourself what part of the human body best reveals a trusting nature? The eyes. Your photo, for any social network, needs to be high quality and high resolution, so your eyes can be the focal point of the photo. Within seconds, buyers will skim their emails and social messages, and look at related social profile photos. Within seconds, their subconscious minds will determine if you're trustworthy or not. Are you going to defy evolutionary law and post a grainy, camera-phone version of yourself? I hope not! Take a moment to have a picture taken with a clear backdrop that will take the focus off the environment and place the focus on your eyes and smile.

YOUR LINKEDIN HEADLINE IS YOUR ELEVATOR VALUE STATEMENT

We've all heard of an elevator pitch that takes only 30 seconds to summarize and articulate our value. The LinkedIn headline is the exact same thing. It is not a place to repeat your job title again at the top of your profile. Your buyer doesn't care that you're an account manager, sales executive, or customer success specialist. They would never Google one of these titles. In fact, many buyers have a visceral reaction to sales professionals; you're actually making that first impression even more difficult on yourself.

The best way to start creating a LinkedIn headline that resonates with a buyer is to play the elevator pitch game with yourself. Pretend you stepped into an elevator and a senior buyer standing beside you presses the tenth-floor button and, at the same time, bumps into you. As he apologizes, he asks you, "What do you do and how do you add value in your job?" You only have one sentence to respond, so you blurt out a sentence that summarizes some or all of the following:

4. Who you help
5. How you help
6. Why you help better than others

I personally change up my LinkedIn headline on a quarterly basis to experiment and try new things. But ultimately, my value proposition evolves. Here is my LinkedIn headline at this time:

> The "Company of Record" for Social Selling | Digital Integration across your sales and marketing org | Sales for Life

Make note that you'll want to include your company name at the back of the headline. Nothing is more frustrating to buyers than when they see your photo and headline in a small summary, but have no idea where you work.

THE LINKEDIN SUMMARY COMPLETES THE STORY

Buyers won't surmise enough information about you from a photo and headline, so they'll naturally gravitate to the largest block of focused detail, the LinkedIn summary. The vast majority of sales professionals have left this section blank, but they're missing a huge opportunity to contextualize their story.

Start by crafting an expanded value statement that extends from your headline. Ensure this value statement is only a few sentences long, as the human eye likes digesting comic books, not novels. This is your opportunity to outline *how* you solve problems and for *whom*. Within the next block of text, leverage examples of success. Personally, I love video, so feel free to add supporting assets to capture the story you want to tell (grab video from your corporate YouTube channel as an example). Buyers want to read your summary and have a clear picture that you've solved problems for companies just like theirs. Tell brief stories; your corporate client success web page is a great start because these stories are already public facing.

Next, focus on outlining a clear call to action for your buyer. Remember that most of your buyers are not first-degree LinkedIn connections, so you need to make it dead simple for a second- or third-degree buyer to reach you.

Finally, because LinkedIn, Twitter, and other social platforms are websites, they're subject to search engine optimization. That means that the more value readers place on a web page (traffic is an example metric), the higher Google will place that website in a search result. Your LinkedIn profile can act as your personal website, and keywords embedded into your profile can add value to your SEO. Those keywords at the bottom of your summary act like tags that describe features, functions, benefits, strategies, and industries you serve.

EXAMPLE: JAMIE SHANKS'S LINKEDIN SUMMARY

Welcome to Social Selling Mastery—as we've built the world's largest social selling training curriculum, used by over 60,000 sales professionals.

I am part of the world's largest network of social selling training experts, who contribute their best practices to our central social selling content. How do I help?

- Build a social selling ecosystem (digital transformation) process in companies that changes the sales behavior forever.
- Empower sales and marketing professionals to drive new business using content and engaging conversations on LinkedIn, Twitter, and other social tools.
- Create measurement systems within our customers' CRM, so leaders can measure learning behavior translating into sales outcomes.

See how these companies now drive more sales opportunities with social selling:

Intel, GE Capital, Sprint, SAS, CA Technologies, Thomson Reuters, Oracle, ADP, Kronos, Teradata, HUB International, Humana, Concentra, HireRight, MTS Allstream, TIBCO, Spotfire, American Express, XO Communications, New Horizons, SagePay, D&B, Direct Energy, EDC, Vision Critical, Cision, uSamp, Tata Communications, SilkRoad, Kofax, ReadyTalk, Entrust, Deltek, Meru Networks, ConnectFirst, InContact, Direct Energy, ON24

Contact Me:

Email | jamie@salesforlife.com

Phone | 905-502-5512 x4009

Social Selling | Sales Performance | LinkedIn Training | Twitter Training | Social Selling Training | Hootsuite Training | Social Media Training | Sales Enablement | Sales Enablement | Sales Effectiveness | Sales Training | Sales Methodology | Sales Talent | Sales Management Training | Sales Agency | Crowdsourcing

LINKEDIN RECOMMENDATIONS VALIDATE YOU'RE TRUSTWORTHY

Recommendations have been part of selling longer than I've been alive. I've been in the front lobbies of companies where they showcase their client recommendations on the walls like trophies. Why do this? Simple. You feel more comfortable that you're in the right hands.

The personal recommendation via LinkedIn is highly valuable to be able to leverage for future sales opportunities, but to master gathering recommendations, you first need to understand and master the law of reciprocity. It's simple; we all learned it as children, yet we forget its virtues later as adults.

The law of reciprocity is: When someone does something nice for you, your hard-wired human nature determines that you do something nice for them in return.

Leverage this principle to first recommend a buyer after a great encounter, engagement, project, expereince, and so on. Don't ask for a recommendation first; give a recommendation. The system in LinkedIn will give the buyer the opportunity to return the favor. Be very mindful of timing as time is of the essence. Deliver that recommendation in real time, not six months after the engagement. The magic of the moment is then lost. Take advantage of a positive experience in the moment and even call it out. Let the buyer know that when you get back in the office, you'll be sending him or her a recommendation. Make it a next step in your communications plan.

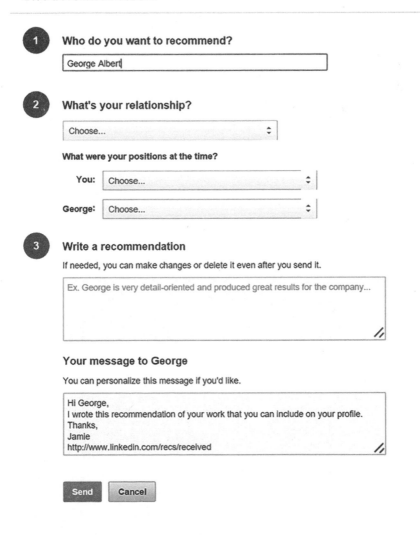

Give a recommendation

1 **Who do you want to recommend?**

George Albert

2 **What's your relationship?**

Choose...

What were your positions at the time?

You: Choose...

George: Choose...

3 **Write a recommendation**

If needed, you can make changes or delete it even after you send it.

Ex. George is very detail-oriented and produced great results for the company...

Your message to George

You can personalize this message if you'd like.

Hi George,
I wrote this recommendation of your work that you can include on your profile.
Thanks,
Jamie
http://www.linkedin.com/recs/received

Send   Cancel

CHAPTER 8

Find

Socially Surround a Buyer and the Buying Committee

The only difference between a mob and a trained army is organization.

—Calvin Coolidge

Organization has been and always will be a critical part of sales success. I also find it to be one of the first stumbling blocks for sales professionals, and a reason why social selling doesn't accelerate their business like it should. There are so many things to do socially, but where do you start?

MAPPING YOUR SALES WORLD TOWARD YOUR SOCIAL WORLD

We all leverage some sort of customer relationship management (CRM) software to keep ourselves organized. CRMs are meant to be the backbone of our buyer information, activities, and next steps.

Your first task is to get organized socially, and plot a course to improve your social reach. Your sales universe is mapped in your

CRM, assigned to your name. Note: If you're a sales professional who deals with inbound leads with no dedicated account assignment, don't worry, the same principles apply to you. Your CRM data is a collection of contacts, but your social network(s) are a collection of relationships. Your goal is to merge these worlds together so they mirror each other in a 1:1 ratio.

Total Social Capitalization Potential = CRM Data

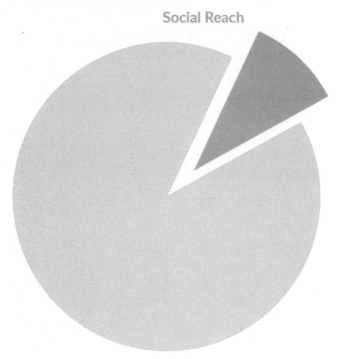

Social Reach

As an example, if you have 50 named accounts in your territory, and you know that on average there are 5.4 buyers in each account (statistics according to the CEB), you have approximately 250 buyers that you need to *find* for your social relationships.

We cover how to tactically find these buyers later in this chapter, but as a general principle, that is your ultimate goal. Why keep a collection of data points in your CRM, if you're not going to actively monitor and nurture that same buyer in a social environment? Socially surrounding a buyer is the intersection of *finding* the buyer, *organizing* the information about the buyer, and then taking a sales *action*.

All of this planning and organizing of social relationships is important to be able to execute a quick-fire sales action.

As you begin expanding your socially surrounding mindset from one buyer to many buyers, you become ready to start thinking bigger.

MULTIPLYING *FIND*: SOCIALLY SURROUNDING A BUYER

Socially Surround – Order of Operations

Finding a buyer goes far beyond the individual contact. Socially surrounding a buyer is about understanding their micro and macro ecosystem, and uncovering answers to the following:

1. Who else in the business unit will be part of the buying committee?
2. Are there other divisions or related corporate entities, and people within those organizations, I need to know?
3. Who influences all these people? Stockholders, industry experts, competitors?

TACTIC 1: FIND BUYERS' PROFILES ON LINKEDIN, TWITTER, AND GOOGLE

Whoever your buyer is, whether it's an inbound lead or assigned multi-national account, you need to find his or her information on major online and social platforms. For the illustration of this process, we concentrate on LinkedIn, Twitter, and Google, but please leverage platforms that best find buyers in your regional market.

Creating an organizational chart of a buyer's universe might sound complex, but it's worth the minutes of planning versus hours of agony months later when you find out you've missed critical people in the sales process. Whether you use a free, premium, or Sales Navigator LinkedIn account, the same principles apply: *Find* the buyers! LinkedIn Sales Navigator makes this process much quicker as you can search an account name, and quickly highlight applicable buyers (i.e., contacts, but LinkedIn calls them "leads").

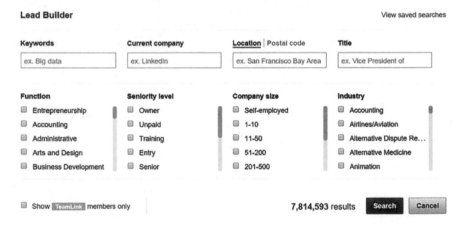

If you're leveraging a free or premium LinkedIn account, you'll need to begin mastering Boolean searching. This will become a transferable skill that you can use on other social platforms, as they all search using this logic. There are entire books written on this topic, but I summarize what you need to know in the following list. These are the five key elements to Boolean search terms that you can leverage within a LinkedIn advanced search, a Twitter search, or a Google search.

1. **OR:** Word A *OR* Word B applies (mutually exclusive). For example, you would use this when searching for all your named accounts.
   Oracle OR IBM OR SAP OR TIBCO OR EMC

2. **AND:** Word A *AND* Word B work only together. An example is a search for a person's title by seniority *and* job function.
Director AND Sales

3. **" ":** Enclose your search term in quotation marks to capture the entire phrase. Without these quotation marks around the entire phrase search results will include profiles that include any of the words.
"Thomson Reuters," "Royal Dutch Shell"

4. **():** Use parentheses to capture a series of thoughts in order of operations. This ensures an entire string of search ideas is not jumbled, allowing Boolean logic to solve the elements within the parentheses first before moving to other elements.
(Director OR VP OR Chief) AND Sales

5. **NOT:** Use this only when a search returns undesirable data about a company, job function, or keyword. NOT will exclude whatever elements you want from that search.

Title: VP Sales   *Company: NOT IBM*

Mastering this Boolean logic will pay dividends in the accuracy of your LinkedIn, Twitter, and Google searches (including Google Alerts) for companies and the buyers who work at these companies.

There are dozens of ways to manipulate the search criteria on LinkedIn to meet your specific needs. For some of you reading this book, you may focus on specific geographic regions, while others work within very specific industries. There are hundreds of videos on YouTube, blogs on Google, and help features on LinkedIn that will provide guidance on those subtle details. My objective here is to guide you to a sales outcome, which is to quickly *find* your desired accounts in all applicable social platforms, and then isolate the buyers (decision-makers, champions, influencers, and industry experts) who control that market. This is the future social ecosystem you need to focus on!

After you've found all of your targeted accounts and buyers, to which your CRM information and social networks could be mirrored in a 1:1 relationship, it's time to save and tag this information in your social networks. World-class sales professionals know that success is about time optimization, and saving all this social data, which provides you with real-time information, is critical for speed-to-revenue.

In Google, you want to capture and save this information in Google Alerts. Google Alerts will provide you a daily email digest of information from around the world (or specific to your needs if you filter) on any company, person, or subject matter you need. I highly recommend you create Google Alerts for the following:

4. All named, or top accounts
5. Key executives at the accounts you're following
6. Competitors to your to top accounts
7. Industry keywords that are critical to your buyer

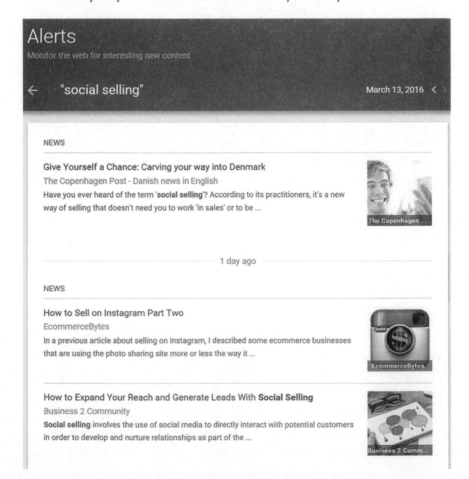

Repeat this process in Twitter, using Twitter lists. I've found that Twitter overexposes me to conversations and content that mean very little in helping me sell. Twitter lists help me cut through the noise and tag, save, and access the Twitter accounts and conversations that I care about. Similar to creating Google Alerts, I develop file folders to house:

8. All named, or top accounts
9. Key executives at the accounts you're following
10. Competitors to your to top accounts
11. Industry analysts or thought learners who provide excellent insights into my buyer's world

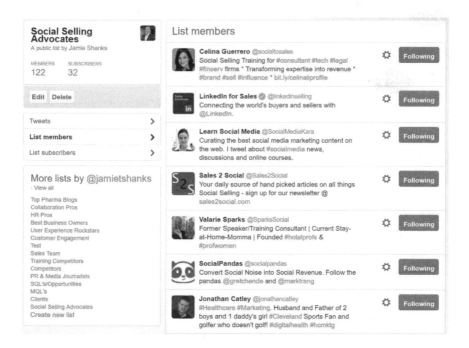

I then find Twitter handles for the accounts, buyers, and/or industry experts who are applicable, and I click "Add to Twitter List" for each of them. After completing this exercise, I have all my CRM data and social networks aligned in a 1:1 tracking position.

On a daily basis, I spend a few minutes to review the newly emailed Google Alerts, scroll through the Twitter lists, and check my LinkedIn news and shares for any information I can use to have a more informed conversation with my buyers. I've created a radar station for my buying universe.

TACTIC 2: CREATE TRIGGER-BASED ALERTS THAT SOCIALLY SURROUND YOUR BUYER

Once you've socially surrounded your buyer and his or her buying committee, it's time to begin commercializing any valuable social trigger.

I'll always remember how I developed a keen understanding of the importance of fob changes as a social trigger. First, when I was a young sales professional in commercial real estate, there was a senior broker named Cam McDonald who was one of my mentors. I used to see him collect the résumé of every CFO in Toronto whom he met and organize them on his desk. One day, I asked him, "Why do you have these resumes? We're in commercial real estate." He wisely said, "There is nothing more personal to these CFOs than helping them transition to a new role. If I help them in that transition, they'll be clients of mine for life. I first broker career help, then I broker real estate." It blew my mind. I'll never forget it. Then in 2012, I meet Craig Elias, author of the book *Shift Selling*. Craig's entire sales career is dedicated to teaching sales professionals that specific internal or external triggers, centered on a particular buyer, open sales opportunities fast! Craig talks about six major triggers, but I've always been fascinated with one: the job change. I quickly realized that LinkedIn is providing me these job change triggers every day, from around the world, about hundreds or thousands of buyers in my target market. The question is: Do you know how to harness this information?

I recommend you learn to master one or more of these three search criteria types, which will provide you with new leads or insights as to job movement within your target markets.

1. Advocates Search

To me, and most of our clients, this is the single most important trigger to opening new accounts. Its premise is based on previous customer success stories. This search is simple in principle. Your organization has many client success stories, yet every day, week, and month, there are scores of buyers leaving those accounts and going to new companies. This is where the opportunity lies! In the first 90 days of a buyer landing at a new company (this, of course, assumes the buyer matches your Ideal Customer Profile), he or she naturally wants to make a splash. Making a splash is typically done using the same people, process, and technology that made that buyer successful at his or her previous company . . . *which is your solution*! These buyers know your value and your solutions application, so this is your opportunity to remind them of those successes.

Within the regular LinkedIn application (this feature is not currently available in LinkedIn Sales Navigator), build an advanced search based on your previous customer success stories. Under the company tab, begin placing customers' names:

Oracle OR "Thomson Reuters" OR SAS

As you begin filling in that information, a box will appear below offering four types of employment history: Current OR Past; Current; Past; Past NOT Current. You're interested in "Past NOT Current" as you're looking for buyers who *no longer* work at the companies where you had your biggest client success stories. You can then focus this search by selecting other essential variables such as title, geography, and so on to make the search more refined to your needs.

The results are *Glengarry Glen Ross* leads! The hot leads that come with a golden bow on top of the package! These are buyers who have used your solutions in the past, know your value, and are in a position to purchase at their new organization. Leveraging the "Saved Search" button, you can have this information automatically updated for you on a daily or weekly basis. New leads will be raining in.

2. New Hires and Appointed Leaders Search

The exact opposite search to the advocates search can also be built and, in fact, LinkedIn Sales Navigator was designed specifically for this function. The goal is to alert you whenever a new hire or appointed job change happens within a specific account. I find this search is excellent for account-based sales professionals, whose responsibility is to absolutely socially surround an account and know all its subtle changes.

In the same example as before, you search for accounts:

Oracle OR "Thomson Reuters" OR SAS

In the free LinkedIn system, you select "Current" under the company. LinkedIn Sales Navigator does a great job of highlighting and tagging the account for you, and naturally tags "Current."

The goal here is simple. You may already know who the CFO, CMO, and CIO of Thomson Reuters are, but are you actively monitoring the job changes of both these key functions and any future hires? Are there any departmental changes? Do you know about the job changes at the senior manager and director levels? One major piece of advice is to monitor the department of your buyer, not just the decision-makers. You'll miss the functional users and champions for your solution.

This search may not yield results for weeks as the company may have a period of job stability. But like any great alert, it provides you contextual information when you're not paying attention. You do not want to miss a new director of information technology who could be six weeks from now and become a major champion or mobilizer.

3. Let's Find New Opportunities Search

Finally, for any presales professional who has been assigned a geography, industry, or vertical territory where named accounts haven't been predefined, this search is for you. Similar to monitoring new hires and appointed leaders, you want to see every ideal buyer in your target market changing jobs! This becomes like a stock ticker of information as you watch CFOs or IT leaders join companies within your territory or you see 37 new HR leaders in new roles across the financial services vertical. The search variables are plenty, but keep your goal in mind. You want to monitor buyers taking new jobs and companies that offer a new opportunity (or, perhaps, help you rekindle conversations with an existing customer) because you now have something contextual to discuss: How are you, the buyer, going to be successful in your new role?

TACTIC 3: PROFILING A BUYER'S SPHERE OF INFLUENCE

The most important revelation I ever had as a sales professional is the same revelation that rocketed Sales for Life into the social selling world. This sales concept had me selling stories that directly related to a buyer's sphere of influence. The concept is very simple. Buyers (who are just people) only really care about information that has a direct, first-degree proximity to their own lives. I recognized that sales professionals, including myself, were guilty of highlighting client success stories to future buyers, only to watch their eyes glaze over with disinterest. Their disinterest wasn't in me or the story; the disinterest was in the lack of proximity to that buyer's life. As humans, we experience this disconnect when 10,000 people perish in an earthquake on the other side of the world, but our sadness is just a fraction of what we feel when a loved one passes away. Stories only matter if you can picture yourself in that story!

Thus, I designed a framework for the sphere of influence. In the center of the image is your client success story. The main question is: Who else would care about this story?

At a corporate level, if my client success story is Company ABC, I must find the following buyers who are within one degree of proximity to that story:

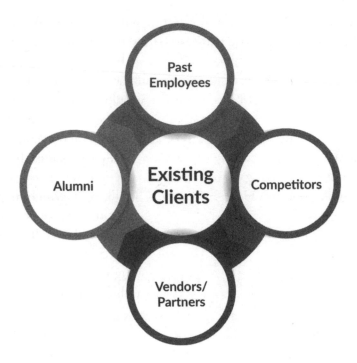

1. Past or current employees of the company in the buyer story
2. Competitors to the example in the buyer story
3. Vendors, partners, or businesses that interact with my client on a frequent basis

In the previous section, we spoke about triggers relating to job changes, which are an excellent element of the sphere of influence. Tell the story of Company ABC to people who have left Company ABC to join Company DEF, because they can most relate to the story. It is a common practice for sales professionals to take a story of Company ABC and sell that story to new divisions within the same Company ABC, especially for multinational corporations. Selling these same stories to competitors is nothing new to sales. We all know instinctively that a competitive story can be the catalyst to pushing a buyer off his or her status quo, and taking a discovery call with you to talk details of his or her competitor's success. At the time of this publication, our sales team is conducting "Content Audits" in a sphere of influence around our customer base. We're showcasing a comparison study of our customer's sales team versus their nearest competitors when it comes to sharing insights with their buyers on LinkedIn. After the data is packaged into a visual story, these digital insights are highly compelling to a VP of sales or marketing who can immediately see the challenge he or she is facing against his or her competitors.

The area within the sphere of influence I'd like to highlight is outside of the corporate level and drills into your personal sphere of influence. That can be best bottled and monetized using LinkedIn's alumni search function. The LinkedIn alumni search, located under My Network, is a tool that allows you to highlight all previous attendees of your college or university (including military institutions).

This tool allows you to segment the data by graduation date ranges, cities, job function, current employer, and so on. As an example, I did my undergraduate bachelor of commerce degree at the University of Ottawa in Canada. At the time of this publication, there are approximately 102,000 people who have tagged themselves as University of Ottawa alumni. While that macro data is of little value to me opening a new door at a prospective account, it's how I leverage this tool that determines my ability to road map relationships.

The University of Ottawa is a large (by Canadian standards) doctorate school with more than 30,000 attendees per annum. While I feel that the school isn't rich in campus culture or alumni brotherhood, it does have some incredible partying. This is due to its proximity to downtown Ottawa's party scene and the densely populated "student ghetto housing," which made it a hot spot for house parties that spilled over to bars. The main bar that students frequented after house parties was Fathers & Sons, and generations of University of Ottawa alumni giggle upon hearing the bar's name, even ten years after graduation. We all have great memories of that joint. But herein lies the value of the sphere of influence: Each University of Ottawa alumnus has a shared life experience with me . . . drinking at Fathers & Sons. Now, leveraging this LinkedIn alumni tool, I can isolate companies in various markets that I'm keen to penetrate. There are thousands of organizations that have University of Ottawa alumni on their payrolls. I may have a shared life experience with someone at my prospective account! What the LinkedIn alumni search also shows me is a list of my ideal buyers within an account, whom I don't know personally, but I potentially have two elements in common with them:

1. Shared life experience from Ottawa.
2. A common trusted person because, while we're second-degree connections, we have a common first-degree connection whom both of us know well. This common person can be a great bridge for our conversation.

Travis Burke

Corporate Development,
Partnerships & Alliances.
Globally.

Toronto, Canada Area

'00

According to Sales Benchmark Index, you are 4.2 times more likely to open this door due to a previous relationship or introduction, than you would with your traditional cold message.[1] This is prime referral-based selling. You can unlock accounts that you previously never thought possible to penetrate because people have a shared life experience with you.

---

[1] Sales Benchmark Index. "How to Make Your Number in 2010: A Sales Strategy You Can Execute," 7th annual research report, 2013. Available at: https://business.linkedin.com/content/dam/business/sales-solutions/global/en_US/c/pdfs/linkedin-sbi-sales-research-report-us-en-130920.pdf.

CHAPTER 9

Educate

Leveraging Content to Shape a Buyer's Journey

Education is the kindling of a flame, not the filling of a vessel.

—Socrates

While trigger-based selling may not happen each day (as there might not be a new trigger to start a new conversation), insight-based selling never stops. Self-education, so you can better serve your buyer, is the first stage to insight-based selling. I would be lying if I said that changing a sales professional's self-education patterns will be easy. It's not. In fact, this is typically where sales professionals fall down, reverting to their old playbook, and neglect social selling over time. Education takes time, which we in sales never seem to have enough of. Unfortunately, you can't truly understand your buyer and gain your buyer's mindshare, unless you provide new ideas that truly push him or her to think differently.

Buyers are looking for teachers and consultants, not order-takers or caretakers of the relationship. This is perfectly articulated in

Forrester's recent study called "Death of a B2B Salesperson."[1] A buyer is looking for you to provide a road map from problem to nirvana, then present best practices to mitigating risk and cost along the journey. Please understand that a buyer is conducting due diligence without you, gathering information from Google, competitors, industry analysts, and peers. If you think your corporate marketing material is the only information necessary to capture a buyer's mindshare, you're already behind the eight ball in that account! When you interact with a buyer on the phone, email, voicemail, conference call, and in person, you need proof of your claims. You need to validate the data, facts, and outcomes that you're claiming give you an edge over competitors, benchmarking against industry best practices. Your buyer is looking for this level of transparency and agnostic approach from you. The days of shilling bullshit are over!

How do you begin the education process? By acquiring insights and by delivering insights.

ACQUIRING INSIGHTS

We have already covered sources for great insights, such as Google Alerts, but I want to focus on articles, blogs, ebooks, infographics, and videos that contain rich content used to tell great stories. Your options for acquiring insights, then, fall into two categories:

1. Internally driven insights
2. Externally captured insights

Internally Driven Insights

In Chapter 15, we talk about building a world-class internal content library that sales professionals can leverage. I will not spoil the fun,

---

[1] Forrester, "Death of a (B2B) Salesman," April 13, 2015. Available at: https://www.forrester.com/report/Death+Of+A+B2B+Salesman/-/E-RES122288.

but the goal is to have a visually rich library that any sales professional can access that makes it super simple and intuitive to answer the following questions:

- What insights are available for my specific buyer persona?
- Within that buyer persona, my buyer is at X stage of their buying journey. What's valuable for them now?
- Of these very specific insights, perfect for that buyer persona, at that particular stage of their buying journey, what type of assets most resonate with my buyer? Blogs, ebooks, video?

We cover these best practices in great detail, but assuming your team lacks a content library that's robust enough to showcase available content based on that logic, I recommend you start capturing external insights.

Externally Captured Insights

These are insights that are not created by your organization. While they won't necessarily drive inbound leads into your sales funnel (because they lack a marketing-driven call to action), you will be able to gather extremely relevant insights for very specific situations. These insights are still incredible at serving your buyer, regardless of the lack of short-term lead generation opportunities for you. The law of reciprocity will always reign supreme, and your insights shared with buyers today will pay dividends for you in the future.

To start capturing externally facing insights, first find a free content aggregation tool that you prefer. I personally like Feed.ly, but some of you might use Flipboard or Buffer. These tools allow you to tag blog sites from any company, analyst, and industry organization that you feel creates highly valuable content for your buyer. The best blogs to harness are those your buyers are most often reading today. You can find this information using these tools' keyword searches or a quick Google search for "top blog in X industry." As an example, here is a sample list of blogs saved in my Feed.ly account under my social selling category:

Your content aggregator allows you to segment blog sites by categories, which in turn, allows you to have blogs for multiple buyer personas or hot topics in your industry. The tools are the vessel of information, but it's your job to ignite your own flame by reading these insights consistently so you can deliver new ideas to a buyer. As a general rule for myself, I spend 10–15 minutes each morning, as I'm eating breakfast, to find valuable insights that I think will be great to share socially in a 1-to-1 context with a specific buyer based on a conversation that we've had.

While your social aggregator is a content vessel, it can often resemble a dumping ground, rather than a highly organized machine. That's why tools like Feed.ly integrate nicely with content organizing tools such as Evernote or Pocket, or purchase the premium version of Feed.Ly to tab and store articles. These tools are meant for you to extract and tag the articles that you'll use over and over in conversations; you can save and categorize them for simple organization. As you start leveraging these tools, you'll begin to ask yourself: "What is the best tagging system to keep the articles highly relevant when I'm searching?" I recommend you use a simplistic version of what we cover in the marketing Chapter 14, "What Is the Current State of Your Lead Factory?" We use three simple categories: why, how, and who.

Why?	How?	Who?
Do I have a problem?	Do I solve the problems?	Do I choose to help solve the problem?

Your buyer's journey, and your sales process for that matter, can be carved into three fundamental questions that a buyer asks:

1. Why do I have a problem?
2. How do I solve that problem?
3. Who do I choose to help solve my problem?

Within your content aggregator tool, create a foundation tab for each question (why, how, and who), and tag each article you save with one of these labels. You can add layers of granularity if you have many articles saved and need to be hyper specific. You can create additional tags for buyer personas (CFO, CIO, CMO), so now your insights are searchable by buyer journey stage and persona. The better you organize these insights, the more likely you'll spend time ingesting the knowledge and saving these nuggets of gold for future sales conversations.

DELIVERING INSIGHTS

Reading new insights does little if the information doesn't end up in your buyer's hands. This section focuses on sharing these insights in a one-to-many scenario with your social networks. As previously mentioned, the greater your social reach, the greater the impact these delivered insights have on your sales opportunities. This is the first and probably most critical element to social engagement. You must adjust your mindset to inherently believe that by sharing valuable insights socially, you're helping one or more potential buyers, ever so slightly, day by day. If you compound this education over time, you will place yourself in a much more advantageous spot when one of those buyers is ready for the next steps. I recommend you begin changing your social behavior by sharing insights manually on LinkedIn and Twitter, leveraging the share buttons or manually posting the content on your home screen.

The only way sharing insights will become habitual, and ultimately, valuable for your buyer is if you deliver insights on LinkedIn and Twitter on a daily basis. The average LinkedIn user is only on the platform for a few hours a week, so you must create exposure with a minimum viable omnipresence. Even at one article posted per day, the probability that a buyer noticed the article you shared is quite low. This is why we recommend content distribution tools such as Hootsuite *only after* you see value in sharing insights manually. I'm a firm believer that if you don't see the value of sharing insights manually, pouring rocket fuel on a dead flame is going to do very little.

On an individual basis, you can leverage tools such as Hootsuite (or its Google Chrome extension Hootlet) to accelerate your sharing process. I use Hootlet because it allows me to click to share content right from the article's website, customize my social messaging, and schedule the article for future sharing times. With minimal effort, I amplify my exposure to a completely different magnitude. I'm a true believer in Grant Cardone's "10X Rule" concept around omnipresence, that you must "burst through obscurity."[2] I recommend that you share a minimum of three insights per day:

1. Before 9 ~AM when your buyers start their day.
2. 12–1 ~PM, during your buyers' lunch period.

---

[2] Grant Cardone, *The 10X Rule: The Only Difference Between Success and Failure*, Wiley, 2011. http://ca.wiley.com/WileyCDA/WileyTitle/productCd -1118064089.html

3. After 5 ~PM. when your buyers are finishing work.
4. Sunday evenings are also perfect, as your buyers are preparing for their new week in a relaxed, highly focused but digestive mindset from their home office.

I particularly recommend sharing insights socially from the *why* category. Create inception, be first, and capture a buyer's mindshare when they're first formulating problems in their mind. *Why-* and early *how*-based insights are best for social sharing as they also help you *fish with a net*. Late *how-* or *who*-based insights are meant for contextual, one-on-one discussions with the buyer; this is *fishing with a spear*. Don't make the mistake of thinking that your company's case studies, *who*-type insights, are going to move your buyers off their status quo to purchase.

In the book *The Ultimate Sales Machine: Turbocharge Your Business with Relentless Focus on 12 Key Strategies*, Chet Holmes cites research that shows that only 3 percent of your target buyers are actively seeking to buy.[3]

The Demand Generation Pyramid

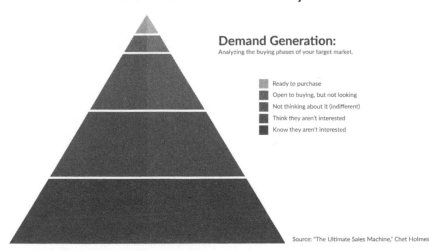

Source: "The Ultimate Sales Machine," Chet Holmes

---

[3] Chet Holmes, *The Ultimate Sales Machine: Turbocharge Your Business with Relentless Focus on 12 Key Strategies,* https://www.amazon.ca/Ultimate-Sales -Machine-Turbocharge-Relentless/dp/1591842158

That means that the vast majority of your buyers haven't accurately identified a problem or formulated an action plan. Show them the opportunity cost of their status quo and the consequences of inaction. Your insights become both your building blocks to a trusted brand and your knowledge-bombing weapon.

CHAPTER 10

Engage

Touching "Every Deal, Every Day" with Social Media

If you don't shoot, you can't score.

—Wayne Gretzky

Selling is like a sport; your success can be distilled to two questions:

1. Did you execute the right volume of activities?
2. Where can you improve the probability that these activities translate into positive outcomes?

Ineffective social sellers, and 99 percent of the so-called social selling experts in my industry, spend way, way too much time socially listening and very little time socially engaging in sales conversations.

Selling is just like hockey; you need to shoot the damn puck *on net* to give yourself a chance to score. Taking one to two shots a game is just not going to do it. In that same vein, I've heard countless sales professionals state that:

1. "InMails don't work."
2. "I tried connecting with that buyer and he never connected back."
3. "I left a comment on her article but she never called me."
4. "I've retweeted their content many times and I get nothing."

   The Wayne Gretzky in me, the guy who's spent more than ten thousand hours mastering my sales craft (and still has a lifetime of learning to do), snickers every time I hear one of these excuses. If one of Gretzky's coaches had deterred him from spending extra time behind his opposing goalie's net, he may have stopped his ground-breaking behind-the-net tactics. In the late 1970s, a few coaches probably thought his tactics were a terrible strategy because the game of hockey had always been played in front of the goalie. Gretzky tried something new and he didn't try it one or two times. He tried it one or two times every period of every hockey game of the thousands of hockey games he played in. The lesson here is, of course, *persistence*, which is a virtue that sales professionals statistically just don't seem to possess. According to SiriusDecisions, a sales professional will make less than two attempts to reach a buyer.[1] Yet ironically, you as a sales professional have most likely been taught the power of the multiple-touch approach. Don't just leverage the same tool (telephone), calling at the same times (5 ~PM) for only two attempts, and expect anything less than average results. Social sellers leverage all the tools in their arsenal in a variety of touchpoint cadences to reach your buyer.

---

[1] September 14, 2015 Hubspot, http://blog.hubspot.com/sales/sales-statistics

WHERE DO I BEGIN?

First, you must agree with Jill Rowley's principle of "every deal, every day," then, agree to approach your target market on a daily basis, isolate a particular account, and ask yourself:

"What can I do today to better serve my buyers? What can I do to help those buyers along their buying journey?"

This selfless reflection demonstrates that you are thinking about your buyers ahead of your own sales process. As you isolate and focus on Company ABC, ask yourself:

"Is there a trigger alert, valuable insight, or referral that can help me start a conversation with this buyer?"

By asking yourself this question, you'll start to devise a plan to approach each buyer. Each buyer will have a different touchpoint cadence based on your last conversation, but the game plan ultimately includes multiple touches. You can plan those touches to come in the form of triggers, insights, and referrals.

GROW YOUR SLICE OF THE SOCIAL-REACH PIE!

In Chapter 8, "Find," you began thinking about how social selling can be leveraged in your total sales universe. This represents all your accounts that you could possibly penetrate in your defined target market. In fancy banker terms, you would call this your market capitalization. As an example, if you have 50 accounts and five people at each account to follow, your market capitalization is 250 people. Since you took the time to find and organize these 250 people from Chapter 8, it's time to grow your slice of the social-reach pie. You want to benchmark the percentage of those people that follow you on Twitter or with whom you have a first-degree connection with on LinkedIn, then devise a touch point sequence to improve that ratio.

Your engagement on LinkedIn could come in the following forms:

1. LinkedIn connection request to become a first-degree connection
2. LinkedIn group message to start a conversation
3. LinkedIn InMail to start a conversation
4. Share or commenting on LinkedIn content to start a conversation

Your engagement on Twitter could be the following:

5. Mentioning a buyer as you share an article
6. Retweeting or favoriting an article your buyer has shared and adding context with your comments
7. Directly messaging a buyer (I love using a Twitter video).

We'll explore these engagement ideas, but first I need you to embrace the philosophy of *never sending a naked message*. Soak this idea into your bones, along with the law of reciprocity, and social selling will become instinctive for you. *Never send a naked message* means never communicate with a buyer without adding value. The currency of value today is typically content. Whether that touchpoint is to qualify a lead, nurture an unresponsive buyer, or follow up on a defined task, *every* communication is an opportunity for furthering your buyer's knowledge base. It makes my blood boil when I see sales professionals not leave a call-to-action voicemail to drive the buyer to look for an email that contains a great insight. I don't understand how they don't see every communication with a buyer as one more opportunity to increase that buyer's knowledge base. Do you think that by leaving voicemails each week, week after week for three months, that a buyer is any more knowledgeable about you and your solution? Not at all, so start leaving digital value on *every* touch point!

SOCIAL ENGAGEMENT: YOUR TOUCHPOINT CADENCE

Each social platform offers a uniquely different value proposition for engagement. I find I leverage each tool in a completely different way.

As an example, Twitter is great for real-time engagement with buyers on their mobile phones. I find tweets, more than LinkedIn posts, gain buyers' attention via mobile phone, but a conventional tweet offers little room for contextualizing a valuable message because you have only 140 characters. This is why I use Twitter in two ways: (1) to leverage a tweet to drive to a call to action for better contextualizing, either through a follow-up LinkedIn message or email; and (2) to leverage Twitter's direct video option that allows you to record a 30-second video tweet via mobile phone. The latter method is an incredible opportunity to leave a digital voicemail. While the purpose of your engagement could be to drive a secondary message (email or LinkedIn message), your video message would be highly contextual and unique. Twitter is imperfect and has been accused of "selling in a vacuum of thought leaders, not buyers." I still find that its ability to reach a buyer directly is far faster than any other medium. Look at what the content buyers are sharing. Is there a valuable statement you can make on their content that will garner their attention? Better yet, is there content that you can share and mention to buyers, helping gain their attention? I think too many sales professionals and social media *experts* spend far too much time thinking about engagement etiquette and forget that selling is a contact sport. Any day of the week, I'd choose a sales professional who will try and experiment rather than one who hesitates because of potential etiquette.

Time To Socially Surround The Account

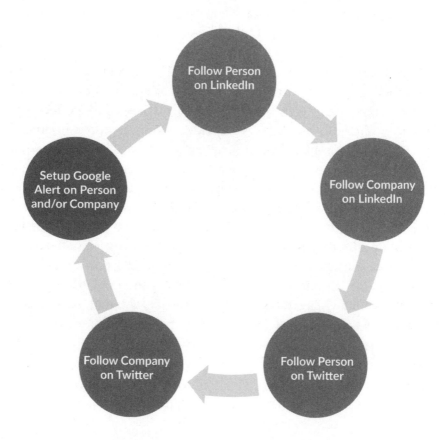

LinkedIn offers you the largest variety of engagement opportunities. Some of these engagements are passive, such as LinkedIn connection requests, but don't discount their value. Remember, your goal is to mirror your CRM information with your social networks and become a first-degree connection with these buyers, allowing for far greater collaboration. Yet, to execute this step without risking rejection or the dreaded *request limbo*, you need to bring active engagement via other

LinkedIn means and use active engagement to lead with value. Here, you have three options:

1. LinkedIn group messages
2. LinkedIn InMail
3. Share or comment on their LinkedIn content

1. LinkedIn Group Messages

You may not have realized that every group you're a part of, each housing thousands of members, allows you the ability to communicate with these members for free! Well, yes and no. As of the date of this publication you are limited to 15 messages per month. Even so, this offers you the ability to join groups that your buyers need and to segment the membership directory and engage in a direct conversation as if you were a first-degree connection. Remember your primary philosophy: Never send a naked message! Remember your primary goal: Add enough value in the first message so that buyers will see value in your next passive engagement through a first-degree connection. Of course, your ultimate goal is to turn this online relationship into an offline business opportunity, but let's not get too far ahead of ourselves. You're leveraging the LinkedIn group message function to kick-start insight-based conversations with a buyer to whom you demonstrate value, and to drive a call-to-action to a next step. I've leveraged this function when I wasn't a LinkedIn Sales Navigator user, and had limitations on my monthly InMail.

2. LinkedIn InMail

LinkedIn group messages and LinkedIn InMail serve the exact same purpose, to kick-start a conversation. You're messaging cadence and call-to-action is also exactly the same. A common question is: "Can an InMail be used to drive a cold conversation to a warm one and lead to an offline discovery call?" Of course! Around the world, thousands of meetings a day are secured this way. But you're also seeking to become a world-class social seller, who understands that selling is also a long-tail game, not just short-tail lead generation. I follow Gary Vaynerchuk because he does an excellent job helping entrepreneurs understand the concept of the long tail. You as a sales professional need to focus on the marathon, not the sprint. There are always quick and dirty ways to open new doors, but there are more valuable methods that leave lasting impressions with buyers, and those typically come with future referrals. As the CEB taught us in "The Challenger Sale," "53% of customer loyalty is attributed to a customer's buying experience,"[2] making the buying experience so critical. Start treating your LinkedIn InMails as if you're beginning a valuable conversation at a dinner party, not making a quick remark to someone as you exit an elevator. Intend to create a dialogue with your buyers.

3. Share or Comment on their LinkedIn Content

Beyond one medium or message, creating your awareness happens with omnipresence and by socially surrounding your buyer. Social sellers will incorporate sharing or commenting on a buyer's social posts as a way to kick-start engagement. Great social sellers don't comment because they feel obliged; they comment because they'd like to extend a fresh perspective, or validate the buyer's point of view through a personal story. Your touchpoint cadence should share insights to your entire social network, direct Twitter conversations with buyers, use LinkedIn messages with attached insights to directly communicate with a specific buyer, and comment on a buyer's articles. Those touchpoints are just a portion of your sequence, which also includes emails, voicemails, phone calls, video conferences, personal meetings, and so on. This is how you cut directly into your buyer's center view. You will create omnipresence with your personal brand.

---

[2] CEB, *The Challenger Sale*, https://www.cebglobal.com/top-insights/challenger -sale.html

As I mentioned before, one example of sharing direct insights with a buyer via InMail is the Sales for Life "Content Audit," which we share with VPs of sales and marketing. We strike up a conversation with a sales or marketing VP with a custom three-page document, specific to their sales force, that shows the importance of being first to a sales conversation. To further customize the insight, we illustrate how this approach compares to the percentage of their sales force that's actually shared insights on LinkedIn in the last two weeks. The average sales team may have 25 percent of its sales force sharing insights consistently. This directly shared "Content Audit," which shows exactly which sales professionals are engaging buyers socially, is highly powerful. While we shared the insight directly via LinkedIn InMail, our touchpoint sequence to gain the buyer's attention will use a variety of different approaches over a 30-day period.

MAP YOUR TOUCHPOINT CADENCE

Like a great business plan, you need to plot your touchpoint. Random acts of social in an account will get you nowhere. The statistics from InsideSales.com make it clear that sales professionals are attempting fewer than two touchpoints per buyer, when your business could need 7–10 over 30 days.[3] I find that, in a social world, sales professionals have even less structure and patience to stick to a defined cadence and follow-up process.

Perhaps you have a touchpoint cadence road-mapped in your customer relationship management (CRM) tool, or perhaps it's all in your head. The only difference between this new sequence, and your old sequence, most likely, is adding social touchpoints. A defined cadence isn't about barraging a buyer in all media, all the time, but it does require you to be fluid and to experiment. Experiment with different articles, video messages, and email templates and attachments, voicemail messages directing buyers to a landing page, and so on.

---

[3] Inside Sales Newsletter, "Sales Research Insight: Real Lead Generation Means Speed + Intelligence + Persistence," February 2011. Available at: http://www.insidesales.com/newsletter/Feb2011/companies-failing-at-lead-response.

Whatever you do, *add value* on every touchpoint. When I mean add value, I'm really saying *teach your buyer something new that he or she didn't know yesterday*. I find it gratifying when prospective buyers message me via email, LinkedIn, or Twitter and first acknowledge that it's been my point of view and shared content that has led them to reach out to me.

CHAPTER 11

Develop

Scaling Up Your Social Networks

Succeeding in business is all about making connections.

—Sir Richard Branson

In Chapter 6 we discussed how growing your social networks can provide you with massive opportunities. Jill Rowley is correct in saying that "your network is your net worth."[1] In fact, if you read *Delivering Happiness* by Tony Hsieh, the CEO of Zappos, you'll see that he has attempted to calculate how long it takes to monetize a new personal network. Tony found that it can take upward of two years for a new connection to become a valuable relationship. Why is this timeline important? Because many sales professionals ask themselves, "Which is more important in growing my network? Quantity or

---

[1] Jill Rowley, Hubspot, April 3, 2014. Blog, http://blog.hubspot.com/sales/social -selling-jill-rowley

quality? I don't necessarily have a large target market, so why should I build my network beyond those accounts?"

I've already helped you understand the importance of quality through expanding your social reach, where you will grow your social networks to mirror relationships in your CRM accounts. Now, I'd like you to understand why quantity can also play a large part in your success. I want you to recall our digital newspaper analogy from Chapter 6. Your personal network (think of that as your newspaper subscriber list) is what fuels your ability to virally attract new buyers. When it comes to evaluating new, organic connections, some of the arguments I hear most often from sales professionals are: "They're not a decision-maker," or "They aren't in my target market. Why should I connect with them?" I want you to ask yourself: Where were you two years ago? Who have you met over the last two years who has added value to your life? I also want you to recognize that these potential connections change and grow their authority over time. They change jobs and industries, and can one day be decision-makers in your target market. What about the connections within *their* network? Ignoring a quantity of connections is a huge miscalculation for sales professionals. For all you know, that person asking to connect with you on LinkedIn could golf every Wednesday with the CEO of your top account. That person could have been a university roommate to a future advocate in an account you're chasing. People buy from people, so don't discount the relationships that other people have! Use the following steps to scale up your social networks.

STEP 1: CHECK YOUR DIGITAL VOICEMAILS

Every day, there are people checking out your social profiles. They're curious to learn more about the person who has been consistently sharing valuable insights. It may be a buyer you called last week or a lower-level functional person doing research who works inside an account you've been targeting. Either way, there are people showing expressed interest in you! Every single one of these people has a story and connections, and could help you be one step closer to your goal. Find this list of people on LinkedIn by clicking "People who viewed your profile." Take a moment to write them a custom LinkedIn connection request and add them to your social network. Now, they will be able to much more consistently see the insights you share. Here is your opportunity to build your subscriber base.

STEP 2: CHECK YOUR CONTENT ENGAGEMENT

The same principles apply for checking content engagement as your digital voicemails, except this takes the form of likes, comments, shares, mentions, retweets, and favorites your insights are having on social media. Each one of these people should also be added to your LinkedIn and Twitter networks. These people are already expressing an interest in helping you go more viral.

STEP 3: GROW BY THE POWER OF THREE

Set a goal for yourself to grow your social networks (beyond the required social reach) by at least three people each day. Over the course of 250 business days, there will be 750 new advocates in your network. You will have exponentially changed your exposure and personal brand.

CHAPTER 12

Create a Social Selling Routine

*You will never change your life until you change something
you do daily. The secret of your success is found in your
daily routine.*

—John C. Maxwell

Years ago when I developed the first social selling curriculum Sales for Life taught, it was really an assortment of tips, tricks, and tactics. I didn't appreciate how difficult it was for sales professionals to both digest these tips and incorporate them into their daily routine. Sales professionals, by their very nature, are extremely habitual. They will always tell you that they don't have enough time in the day, so adding something new means taking something out.

I'm far from an expert on sales process efficiency and there are many books written on the subject, so we won't dive too deeply into the subject here. In all of our routines, there is waste. We can always find time to slot in more productive tasks. What I ask is that you find 30–60 minutes each day to execute your social selling routine. You know in your heart you have that time. Give a gift to your future self and start building a social pipeline today. One year from now, you'll be amazed at the opportunities that have come your way.

THE 30–60 MINUTE DAILY SOCIAL SELLING ROUTINE

The path to success is to take massive, determined action.
—Tony Robbins

Creating a social selling routine changed my life. By having every Sales for Life teammate executing his or her routine, it also changed the growth trajectory of our business and, ultimately, changed our more than 250 customers' sales pipelines. This is *the single most important* set of tasks for a sales professional to become an effective social seller. The important piece isn't to follow these same steps in the order they're written. No, the important piece is taking action! The *doing* is the critical part. Within your social selling routine, you will be calling on all Four Pillars of Social Selling Mastery's FEED process—find, educate, engage, and develop.

Find Routine

The better organized you are at developing lists of buyers, the more time you'll save in your routine. In an ideal state, you can rapidly recall any account and contacts from your target market by quickly accessing their information in a social platform. As you recall their information, you think about three elements of social selling—triggers, insights, and referrals—and decide how to best move forward with those buyers. Have there been any triggers that have alerted you to this account? Are there network connections that will help you penetrate this account further? The find routine takes no more than 10 minutes if you've effectively prepared your lists.

Educate Routine

By this point, I hope you've seen the value in self-education and are reviewing insights daily within your social aggregation tool. You're becoming a more informed sales professional, but you're also uncovering excellent insights that your buyer should be consuming. You can take two courses of action:

1. There is an insight that I found that Company ABC would find valuable. I didn't intend to message Company ABC today, but they need to see this.
2. I'm going to seek out a specific insight that will be best suited for the account I identified in my find routine.

This is where you need to be fluid. The following happens to me all the time: I'll wake up with the intent to target Company ABC, but I'll stumble across an article that highlights a myth that Company DEF was arguing about last week. Company DEF has to read this! So I'll adjust my target for the moment.

Engage Routine

This is where the rubber meets the road. Finding buyers on LinkedIn and educating yourself for deeper conversations is excellent, but these won't drive the kind of sales results you need. Passive social selling is for weak sales professionals and so-called *experts*. You are going to engage buyers in conversation every single day. Once you start this routine, you'll recognize very quickly that selling is selling, and how you've been selling via the telephone isn't all that different from the LinkedIn approach. The only difference is that you can remove the *cold* from cold calls because you now have value-driven conversations that are contextual. The most important part to this routine is touch points; there are more of them in addition to following up on previous touchpoints. Great touchpoint cadences are a form of routine. Develop one that suits your target market and don't be afraid to experiment with unique ways of engaging your buyers. I've watched our sales team send personal Twitter videos create a buzz around a buyer's content, or introduce our future buyers to previous customers on LinkedIn. There is no wrong answer. What's wrong is not trying.

Develop Routine

Once every day, typically in the morning, I'll check my digital voice-mails and social engagement on LinkedIn, Twitter, and Facebook. I rarely engage in real-time Twitter conversations during business hours because I find 99 percent of those conversations involve influencers talking in a vacuum. I recommend you keep laser-focused on your typical sales routine, and use 10 minutes each morning to check:

- Who has been on my LinkedIn profile?
- Who liked, commented, or shared on LinkedIn?
- Who mentioned, retweeted, or favorited my insights on Twitter?

I make sure to add these people to my social networks.

The entire social selling routine should not take you more than 30–60 minutes per day. Any longer, and you're detracting from core sales tasks.

The compounding nature of a well-executed social selling routine is staggering to watch. As we grew our sales team, I've seen new hires double their social networks, double their LinkedIn SSI scores, and start creating new opportunities—all within 90 days. Watching sales professionals FEED (find, educate, engage, and develop) their networks is gratifying because I know they've removed other nonessential activity to incorporate this new social selling routine.

In Part Four of this book, written for sales operations and sales enablement, you'll recognize that the social selling routine in Part Two is not enough to scale. This routine is a process for you, the individual sales professional, executing for yourself to hit sales quota. Scale will happen when this social selling routine is executed in unison by all your sales professionals, repeated with consistency and kept accountable each week by measuring current indicators. Keep this is mind as you explore this rest of the book.

Three

BUILDING A LEAD FACTORY WITH DIGITAL CONTENT MARKETING

CHAPTER 13

Why Does Misalignment Exist between Sales and Marketing?

It takes a village to raise a child.

—African Proverb

Men are from Mars; women are from Venus. The struggles that we men have in understanding our female counterparts feels exactly the same as the confusion between sales and marketing departments. Men and woman are human; that's what makes them the same, but many times the similarities end there. The parallels to your sales and marketing teams are most likely just the same. Sales and marketing teams directly touch the customer but, for some reason, the average company just can't find common ground after that.

The African proverb that is the epigraph to this chapter, about raising a child requiring a team effort, should be your eureka moment! I'm telling you right now, greater than 50 percent of the success of a social selling ecosystem within your company is going to start and end with marketing! You might be asking yourself "Isn't this book called *Social Selling Mastery* . . . as in *selling*?" Sales professionals are executing a four-step playbook of FEED (find, educate, engage, and develop), while marketing is the entire back end that supports that playbook. Social selling at the individual sales level, with no unified marketing system, is just a random act of social. This book isn't about what one or a few amazing sales professionals can accomplish. This book is about reaching corporate sales goals as one giant, digitally driven ecosystem. But, to become world-class, you're going to need to peel back your corporate culture onion and understand the root causes for your sales and marketing misalignment or dysfunction today.

EXPLORING SALES AND MARKETING MISALIGNMENT

Marketing teams around the world are busier than ever, scrambling to create digital content to be used for social or email campaigns, sponsored ads, and so on. Many marketing departments have gone through a radical resource change lately as they've pushed out the traditional brochure-building marketers and brought in more digital expertise. So imagine to their surprise, after all this hard work, the sales professionals at their organization all but ignoring their newly produced digital content. In fact, according to SiriusDecisions, "Up to 65% of your marketing team's digital content never makes its way into the customer's hands."[1] SiriusDecisions expands on that statistic to say that in an average enterprise organization that wastage can be valued at $17,400,000. Let's put that into context within your organization. Your digital marketing team will spend about five hours of their eight-hour day in activities that do nothing more than spin its wheels! If you were to ask digital content marketers to use one word to describe how they feel about their place within the organization, they'd say "underappreciated."

If you flip the viewpoint to the sales professionals, they look at the problem with much more cynicism and little remorse for the marketing team. If fact, a sales team looks at its own personal daily activity in binary, black-and-white, results-based evaluation: "Does this create

---

[1] InsightPool, May 18, 2015 https://insightpool.com/top-5-siriusdecisions -takeaways/

sales?" So the sales team's cynicism toward marketing is due to a lack of understanding of how marketing isn't kept to a similar high standard of accountability. Members of your sales team are most likely saying to themselves "I'm not receiving enough leads from market to make my quota!" These sales professionals don't care about a marketer's activity levels unless they can be quantified to influence a sales professional's results. Your sales team can't figure out why it lives under the constant pressure of making sales quota and living by a number when marketing seems to be void of this same level of accountability. *Accountability*—could this be the word that has sales and marketing frustrated at each other?

DOES THIS PROBLEM START WITH BLIND SPOTS?

Marketing has begun leveraging technology to mechanize content distribution and engagement. Many marketing teams have invested heavily into employee advocacy systems (which we explore in greater detail in Chapter 17) only to see sales professionals engagement flatline or decline after launch. Why is this? Marketers will ask themselves in frustration, "Why can't I get my sales team to see the value of content?"

Simply put, sales professionals have no idea that there is a direct or even indirect correlation (known as attribution or influence) among digital content shared with buyers, reaching buyers' hands, and increasing inbound leads. Beyond inbound leads, that same confusion also reaches the top of the sales funnel because sales professionals can't see how content will increase their probability of winning a deal. *Of course, sales doesn't know this.* Salespeople are masters at finding the *path of least resistance*, and only do activities with a what's-in-it-for-me attitude. No matter how you may have tried to explain the conversion funnel to the sales team, it hasn't sunk in! If it had sunk in, you would have sales professionals *flocking* to share digital content with their buyers. You, as a marketer, know this correlation to be true, and you're utterly perplexed that your sales team just doesn't see it. Your sales team will give you golden sales excuses such as "I don't have time." This is sales code for "I don't see value!"

This misalignment on value is actually a data-driven problem. This misalignment is because you have blind spots in the data you share between your departments. These blind spots are perpetuated because sales has an opaque vantage into:

1. "What are you doing back there? Your production schedule, which is supposed to help serve myself and my buyers, is doing very little to help me make quota."
2. "Are my buyers really reading my content? How often and in what order? Just before or after I have a meeting with them?"

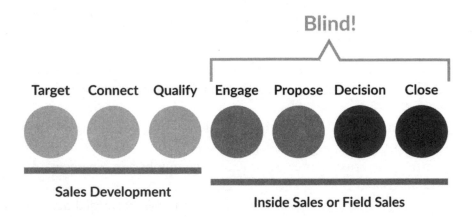

Expanding into the second list item, a buyer is leaving digital fingerprints on your website and on multiple digital assets. This pattern of digital fingerprints is called their content consumption story. The following is an example of how an average sales organization *did not* leverage information about their buyers' content consumption story.

An inbound lead is created, and the marketing team, in partnership with a sales development representative (SDR), will place a call to that lead. A strong SDR would leverage some contextual information about that buyer's digital history, perhaps the ebook he or she downloaded, to become a lead. The SDR has a phone conversation with the lead, and books a discovery call with the prospective buyer that will include a senior sales executive. From the moment that discovery call was booked, in nearly every sales organization I've ever seen, the digital fingerprints of that buyer are not presented to the senior sales executive. Unfortunately, this sales cycle could be 90, 180, or 365 days long, yet the senior sales executive will not have real-time information of that lead's digital fingerprints. It's no wonder sales professionals have little faith in digital content. In their minds, content does little more than create a random set of inbound leads. The sales organization has never been given the intelligence on the indirect influence that digital content is having in shaping a buyer's journey for months and months!

HOW DO KPI MEASUREMENTS PLAY WITH MISALIGNMENT?

Answer these questions aloud:

How are quota-carrying sales professionals measured at the end of a
   year?
The percentage of their quota obtained.

The answer is so simple for sales. It's one number, in a percentage. *Binary accountability.*

Sales professionals are paid against that number, rewarded against that number, given accolades such as President's Club trips against that number, and of course, fired against that number. One number to rule them all. As a sales professional, it's the only thing I care about!

But most marketing departments measure themselves against leads, marketing-qualified leads, sales-qualified leads, sales-accepted leads . . . call it what you'd like. It's a solid leading indicator, but it's not sales bookings. Now, before you blow a gasket and give me the excuse that marketing leaders can't control the *closing* of a sale, I want you to check that impulse at the door. That impulse is the mindset of an individual, not an ecosystem. I said this at the beginning of the book, *synergy* is defined as the whole being greater than the sum of its parts. Marketing leaders need to recognize that they're equal contributors, and equally accountable, to sales success. You are all on *Team Revenue.* Your team will behave based on how it is measured. If you continue to give the team a lagging indicator goal like lead volume, that dictates the behavior you will see. This kind of myopic outlook accounts for only a portion of the ecosystem.

Gaps in Marketing Vs. Sales Goals

HOW DO WE CHANGE OUR MINDSET?

Naturally, throughout this process, we are going to extract objective evidence, plot trends, and create a prescription to completely align marketing to sales quota attainment. But fundamentally, there are a few simple changes I'd like you to make first:

1. Drop the word *content* from your vocabulary.

    Content sounds like you produce widgets, bo-bobs, *things*, while *insights* are a form of intellectual property. You need to inherently believe that the insights your team builds are so valuable that you could charge customers for the knowledge. Your company may have 5, 10, 20 years of market experience. This wisdom is what your customers are buying, not just your solution. Change the way your entire organization talks about insights, and treat these assets like you would a government-registered patent to intellectual property.

2. I'm going to Moneyball our digital marketing.

    Marketing is becoming a numbers game just like sales. Great marketing teams are objectively looking at their production capabilities (like an ad agency would) and the results that is having on sales. Like Moneyball did with baseball, Team Revenue should focus on the micro-elements of a process by establishing a baseline and making incremental improvements to it. If you take this scientific approach to your marketing team, you'll realize you can control everything like a production line of an automobile. You're going to crush your competition when you can identify a few elements within your marketing process that are yielding the highest return, then accelerate that process faster than anyone in your industry. This is only possible when you measure your production throughput and become objective about your resource capacity at a very granular level.

3. I'll make the first move to extend the olive branch.

Yes, as a marketing leader you're a copilot on Team Revenue. Yes, this is a joint exercise. But guess what? I've trained way too many companies to know that sales leaders don't think they need marketing as much as they do. It's you, the marketing leader, who is going to prove objectively that your team is directly and indirectly fueling sales growth. Sales and marketing alignment in world-class organizations is also orchestrated by sales Enablement and sales operations, but the first move to making this happen, I recommend, comes from you.

CHAPTER 14

What Is the Current State of Your Lead Factory?

If you can't measure it, you can't improve it.
—William Thomson, Lord Kelvin

You and I do the same thing every January 1 as a New Year's resolution. We jump on the scales after an overindulgent holiday season and we create a new weight goal for ourselves. What is the key ingredient here in this action plan? We took a baseline measurement of our current weight. For anyone who has tried to lose weight, you know that this baseline measurement is only part of the equation, and it is your future comparable against the lagging indicator months from now. This is why Jenny Craig and other weight-loss programs have you look deeper into the numbers:

- Calories per meal, calories consumed per day
- Calories burned per activity per day

To millions of people around the world, weight loss is like black magic—a series of potions, spells, and rain dances to be done until one day, magically, they fit into smaller sized jeans. Our scientific mind knows, however, that it's actually simple math:

Calories consumed in one week – Calories burned in one week
  = Weight change

If you burn more than 500 calories than you consume in one week, you will lose one pound that week.

Rationally, you would think every weight-challenged individual would take a calorie mathematics course, and BOOM, weight issues around the world would be solved! The problem is that people get caught up in the art, not the science, of weight loss.

Bringing this analogy to marketing teams, digital content marketing around the world is somehow seen as more art than science. Look at your own marketers. They know *how* leads are created; they know *how* digital insights fuel those leads, but they've never taken the time to engineer a model to achieve specific goals—well at least not sales goals.

Just like our weight-challenged friends, your marketing people must weigh themselves and take a production inventory as a baseline. Please make sure your marketers are not just looking at your past library of assets and saying "We have 500 blog posts," or looking at your lead volume for last year and saying "We hit 132 percent of our leads goal" because that's like saying "I'm 195 lbs." So what? Is that good or bad? Compared to what? How agile am I to change that weight? Does that leave me in a health risk?

To start this process, you should collect three elements to establish your baseline:

1. **Sales Quota:** What does a sales professional on your team think is marketing's direct contribution to their sales quota attainment? What percentage of their personal sales quota will marketing be driving?

2. **Production Volume and Velocity:** How fast can you produce, how often can you produce, and how productive are your current digital assets (segmented into categories by asset type) at supplying

fresh new leads to the sales team? What are the volume and velocity capabilities of your production time? How long does it take to create one blog? How many can you produce in one month?

3. **The Delta:** Reverse engineer the typical sales process to understand the delta between your production capabilities and your sales team's required appetite for new leads. Is there a shortfall based on your new conversations with sales?

Before we start, I want to recognize that this exercise is about fishing with a net, which is creating net new leads via inbound marketing to place into your demand generation waterfall. There are companies that are more focused on fishing with a spear, which has your marketing team targeting very specific accounts to generate sales. I argue that you need to master the foundation of fishing with a net before you go into the high-effort world of spear fishing. In fact, I have a great story about data-driven activity being misaligned with sales quota attainment. My company, Sales for Life, was in the final stages of solidifying a new client project with a company to implement Social Selling Mastery. This technology company has a sales enablement team and that team, alongside sales leadership, was fully bought-in and signed-off on the project. At the eleventh hour, members of the marketing team had some deeper questions for us. We organized a 30-minute call to review these questions. On that call, at least four times, the marketing leader asked me "How many blogs do we need to create to be effective?" Using our weight-loss analogy, it was like he was asking me "How many sit-ups do we need to do to be marathon runners?" The first time he asked this question, I politely responded "I don't know, but you're asking yourself the wrong question. You might not have a volume issue in your insights-creation process, but perhaps, a distribution and engagement issue from your sales team. We'll find out more as we go deeper into the project." Growing more impatient, the marketing leader asked again, "No, you didn't answer my question, how many blogs?" To which I then answered more directly "You're asking yourself the wrong question. You need to understand what production requirements need to be met to achieve your sales team's quota. That's all that matters. That may mean doubling your blog output or that may mean shifting resources to alternative insights such as webinars. The only thing that matters is sales quota attainment, which we're going to help you extrapolate and drive production toward that sale goal." Needless to say, the deal fell apart. I found out weeks later that he thought "I didn't know what I was talking about," which I still laugh at. His mindset was stuck on how much he and his team begrudgingly needed to do, not asking what he could do to make the entire organization successful. Again, he wasn't thinking about the ecosystem. The following steps will help you evaluate the state of your lead factory.

STEP 1: INTERVIEWING THE SALES LEADER

There is nothing more inspiring than seeing the lightbulb go off in a marketer's head after interviewing the sales leader. Most of the time I'm not there to see this meeting live, but when I am, I find it very gratifying. This exercise is an interview in which the marketing team is going to ask the sales leaders a series of simple, straightforward questions. The results, always, always, always, showcase the difference between what sales and marketing deem as success.

You as the marketer can interview the top sales leader, or have your team divide and conquer by interviewing divisional leaders, functional leaders, product leaders. This exercise can never get too granular. The goal is to begin extending the olive branch and show sales leadership that marketing is fully committed to your sales success.

Here is what you want to extract:

1. For your business unit, what sales bookings goal have you committed to for the next 12 months?
2. What is the average sales bookings value per new account won?
3. What percentage of that sales goal, do you think can be sourced and created by a sales professional's own activity versus necessary lead support from sources such as marketing or channel?

These first two questions will allow you to understand the number of new customers that are expected to be won. The third question will help you understand what percentage of those new customers are brought by your marketing team to contribute to their sales goals. We've seen companies that have 80 percent of sales supported by marketing leads and we've seen companies with 0 percent. Either way, you need to hear these facts from the sales leadership. Sales leaders have their neck on the line for sales quota, and perhaps, they didn't consult with you when they gave the CEO, board of directors, or investors that ambitious number. What you might be finding out now, for the first time, is that a percentage of that number is fully expected to be driven from marketing. What you should be left with is a number, the number of *net new customers* your team will capture for sales. Start thinking as though you're all part of Team Revenue and you're all equally accountable!

As your team continues to interview sales leaders, you need to learn more about their sales process and reverse-engineer the probabilities of their average deal. This starts with their won deals, going all the way back to your common metrics, such as leads:

- What is the ratio of proposals sent to new customers?
- What is ratio of opportunities to proposals?
- What is the ratio of sales-qualified leads (SQLs) to opportunities?
- What is the ratio of marketing-qualified leads (MQLs) to SQLs?

You may have the data to fill in probabilities beyond sales leadership such as:

- What is the ratio of leads to MQLs?
- What is the ratio of new subscribers (in your database) to leads?

If you or the sales leader doesn't know these exact numbers, make an educated guess. The goal is that you begin understanding that, for each net new customer the organization wins, someone has to supply many, many leads to achieve these goals. Who is that someone?

STEP 2: INTERVIEW THE MARKETING TEAM

If you managed Jeep's production plant, you would need to pull aside your staff to conduct inventory management. How many bumpers, doors, engines, and transmissions are we building? What is our production capacity?

This factory approach is what's behind our term "insights factory." Your goal is to mass produce the volumes of insights necessary to achieve your sales goals. With this newly minted factory analogy imprinted in your mind, I'd like you to identify the following with your marketing team:

A. What insight types are we currently producing?

   blogs, ebooks, webinars, podcasts, infographics, videos, case studies, and so on

B. For each insight type, how many can we currently build with our resources on an annual basis?

   blogs = 150, ebooks = 12, webinars = 20, and so on

C. For each insight type, approximately how many man-hours are required to develop one insight from that type?

   blogs = 3 hours, ebook = 20 hours, webinars = 6 hours

D. For each insight type, how many net new leads (on average) are created each time we publish?

   blogs = 15, ebooks = 500, webinars = 300

This becomes an eye-opening exercise as you have shined a light on production, no different than Jeep would do on its production line. From these questions, you need to multiply the answer to list item B by the answer to list item D.

$$B \times D = \text{Annual lead volume using current production.}$$

The secondary objective is that answers C and D might show you a few head-scratching numbers. Why do we spend so many man-hours on building insight Type A when, per man-hour, Type B, takes three times less time to produce and achieves five times the number of leads? Think of what we could do with that time savings.

STEP 3: THE DELTA BETWEEN PERCEPTION AND REALITY

Time for the big unveiling.

What is the delta between the volume of leads that the sales team would require in its hands to help ensure they meet their sales quota? Compare this to your current production capacity: Can you produce this volume of leads?

Right about now is when marketers raise their hands and say in a panic, "What I'm hearing, then, is that we need to create more content, is that true?" No, that's not what I'm saying. What I'm saying is that mathematically, unless you adjust the three major levers that *you* can control in digital content marketing, then your sales team will fall short of their sales targets. What are the three levers that you can control?

1. Volume: How many assets can we make?
2. Velocity: At what speed and timeline can we make these assets?
3. Probability: What is the conversion expected from each one of these assets?

If your variables remain constant mathematically based on the information you've collected, your sales team would not reach quota. The good news, though, is that the volume lever is only one of the levers you're going to work to adjust. As an example, if you can change the average leads yield of each of your webinars from 300 net new leads to 500, then you can reduce your webinar volume to accomplish your goals. Or, if you can reduce the man-hours required to create each blog by 50 percent, at 150 annual blogs, then you can save your team 225 man-hours. This will allow you to allocate time to alternative projects and, perhaps, change the velocity of a huge project you've wanted to implement. All of this is possible *only* if you're willing to draw a line in the sand, mark down how you do things today, and plot a course for incremental improvement.

CHAPTER 15

Create High-Quality, High-Quantity Content

You can't build a great building on a weak foundation. You must have a solid foundation if you're going to have a solid superstructure.

—Gordon Hinckley

Everything your marketing team does digitally to support the sales force comes from a foundation. While building the foundation can be laborious and, for many advanced marketing teams, seems elementary, it's critical in building all future sales-facing programs. Don't get frustrated if you feel like you personally are taking a step backward by covering these foundational elements. I want you to remember that your sales leaders, sales professionals, sales enablement, and sales operations find everything about a digital content marketing foundation completely new to them. Alignment between sales and marketing is going to start with communicating how this foundation works and supports us all.

Your insights factory will travel from the foundations of creating insights, all the way to evaluating the engagement of these insights to make informed decisions for incremental improvement. Your insights factory has four pillars:

Marketing CODE

Evaluate   Create

Discover   **Organize**

1. **Create** a foundation for developing new insights at scale. The scaling process will accelerate depending on how much you invest in people, process, and technology.
2. **Organize** insights, which need to be exposed to your buyers fast. This is only possible when you optimize your content library tools to allow the sales team to capture and share insights in a seamless motion.
3. **Discover** innovative guerrilla-marketing ways that you grow sales pipeline. Great marketing teams experiment, measure, rinse, and repeat.
4. **Evaluate** every interaction your insights have with buyers. By compounding these interactions together, you will uncover trends that help you map a prescriptive way to make incremental improvements to your insights factory.

As part of the creation process, a leadership workshop we do with clients is to place their most senior sales and marketing leaders in a boardroom for a few hours with no technology other than pens, sheets of paper, and a whiteboard. The first thing we do is break the sales leaders into small groups, each captained by a marketer who can only observe, not actively participate. For the next 15 minutes, we have the sales leaders in each group draw on a sheet of paper to illustrate what they think is their buyer's journey. Now to contextualize the situation, we typically choose a buyer persona to concentrate on, making the exercise seem more real. For the next 15 minutes, senior sales leaders draw a linear map on a sheet of paper, counseled by their other sales group members. After 15 minutes, the captain draws and explains the group's version of the buyer's journey on a large whiteboard in front of everyone. One by one, teams present their business case for their version. What do you think is the single largest commonality we've found from this workshop? That there are *no* two versions that are alike. *Ever*. That means you have an organization with hundreds or thousands of sales professionals who have no centralized road map for how their buyer is buying. There are, many times, common elements such as *they do research*, but rarely do the senior sales leaders ever draw that stage in the same location as their peers.

STEP 1: CENTRALIZE A BUYER'S JOURNEY

Alignment starts at the literal vernacular level, meaning you need to change your internal language. Every sales professional should be able to instinctively visualize how his or her buyer's decision-making process will progress. This is not a sales process. Your buyer doesn't think about *demos* and *proposals*. Yes, of course, you can have multiple buyers' journeys within your organization—for example, they can be specific to a business unit. However, your goal as Team Revenue is to create a simple-to-understand road map for sales professionals. Here is an example:

Status Quo   Priority Shift   Conceptual Solutions   Vendor Review   Selection

Status Quo: The act of doing nothing. Why make a change? Your biggest competitor is always Status Quo.

Priority Shift: Triggers, whether internal or external, can push new priorities forward. The moment a buyer has the lightbulb go off in his or her head and says, "It's time to change."

Conceptual Solutions: The period of due diligence. Buyers are hungry to learn how to solve their problems.

Vendor Review: Once a buyer understands that a problem can be solved, he or she looks for solution providers who can match to his or her desired criteria.

Selection: When we all make money!

You can use different language, more stages, fewer stages, but what's important is that your sales team understand how your buyers are buying. The team can also become better at pinpointing where a buyer is within his or her specific stage of that journey.

STEP 2: SEGMENT THE BUYER'S JOURNEY INTO SALES-CENTRIC STAGES

Sales professionals will find your 4-, 5-, 6-stage buyer's journey cute, but it won't always help them think like the buyer. Frankly, they just won't remember all the stages. This is when you divide the buyer's journey into three logical subsections and concentrate your teachings on these three elements:

1. **Why** do I have a problem?
2. **How** do I solve this problem?
3. **Who** do I choose to help solve this problem?

Why?	How?	Who?
Do I have a problem?	Do I solve the problems?	Do I choose to help solve the problem?

This is also critical in the backend design of other sales-facing programs such as your content library, employee advocacy platform, and digital fingerprint information from marketing automation delivered to your sales team. We've found that these three simple subsections become the internal language for our customers. Sales professionals can also relate to these three groupings as they have become accustomed to thinking about the sales funnel in thirds: top, middle, and bottom.

STEP 3: KICK-START NEW IDEAS FOR INSIGHTS

In the leadership workshop, we have sales leaders pretend to walk a mile in their buyer's shoes. We first ask a sales leader to name the buyer persona we're all addressing. We give the buyer a name to make this exercise feel real and to point out that we're trying to understand her at a personal level. Sales leaders start to close their eyes and really think of what's ailing that buyer. What is keeping her up at night? Jumpstarting her morning? What problems has she recognized or not recognized? Most likely, these macro problems are much bigger than the solution that you offer. Thinking like your buyer means thinking about core problems. Do not start this exercise by trying desperately to align a buyer problem to your familiar solutions.

One by one, sales leaders approach the whiteboard and write a question that they believe the buyer is asking herself right now. We start in the *why* category to get the team thinking about problems, not solutions. The exercise typically opens the marketing team's eyes in two ways, as paraphrased here:

1. "I didn't realize these are the objections, problems, and macro challenges these buyers are having *long* before they think about our solution."
2. "We have very few to no assets that help address these questions!"

You'll want to create a list of 15–20 questions for both the *why* and *how* categories and map these questions against your current asset inventory. In most instances, from running this workshop, we find that the sales leadership has fueled months of new blogs, ebooks, and webinars that need to be produced by marketing.

STEP 4: DEVELOP AN INSIGHTS COMMITTEE FOR SCALE

The best insights ideas come from your sales force; you just need a better way to mechanize the extraction of these ideas. Welcome to your newly formed Insights Committee. The committee's dual purpose is to supply your marketing team with insight ideas and help create the copy within these insights so it can be immediately deployed to your customers. Don't worry, we won't be getting your sales team to *write* blogs, but we do have an ingenious way to extract the blog copy from them very quickly.

The goal is to have a group of four or five sales professionals (to start) who can bring new insights to the table each month. The best Insights Committee is well rounded to cover topics for each of your buyer personas. Don't underestimate the importance of this committee, as most marketing teams are under-resourced and ill-equipped to produce great insights at scale.

Why will these be great insights? Because unlike your marketing team or outsourced copywriters, your sales team is talking to your buyer *every, single* day. The team hears the objections, pitfalls, challenges, and subtle problems that buyers are really having. Unfortunately, a common marketing instinct is to try to map how a buyer's problem is directly related to your solution. Ask yourself: "Are buyers researching only problems they know have a direct link to your solution?" Of course not! Is your goal to be buyer-centric or product-centric? This is tough for marketers to overcome. The great ones realize that their organization can become the voice and resource for that buyer persona, even if not every insight they produce can directly lead to a solution their company can offer.

STEP 5: CONTENT CALENDAR

Accountability and focus are the keys to great insight development. All of your ideas need to be placed inside a master content calendar (also known as an editorial calendar). This master document is shared with *every* sales professional in the organization to mitigate the question of "When is that infographic you talked about coming out?" It's in the calendar. Most importantly, the calendar is an accountability document that keeps the Insights Committee fueling new insights on schedule. The entire sales organization can also see if Insights Committee members are fulfilling their promises for new ideas.

Your calendar can have these and more tabs:

Submission Deadline—When will the insights be in marketing's hand for copyediting?

Content Type—Are we balancing insights properly? Have we reverted to our comfort zone and created specific insights that we like, even though empirically we know we need a different mixture?

Committee Member—Which team members are responsible for producing which insights? Has there been equal contribution from each team member?

Buyer Persona—Are we creating balance for each persona? Are there gaps we need to fill?

Buyer Stage—Do we focus our attention on lead-generation (*why*) insights or do we need more nurture (*how*) insights?

Call to Action—What are the next steps for the buyer? Where does he or she go next after reviewing this insight?

This document becomes your marketing accountability bible.

CONTENT CREATION BEST PRACTICES

To fuel your insights machine, you have to first develop an internal system to ensure you're developing insights that achieve specific goals. We call these *themes*. Without themes, your marketing team may naturally take the raw ideas from the Insights Committee and continue producing too many insights that drive a similar result. As an example, your company is very strong at taking new insights to develop future blogs, but each blog is written to nurture an existing buyer in your database further and further hrough his or her journey. You've done an excellent job owning the mindshare for buyers in your pipeline, but your blogs do little to attract new buyers. Now, you have a lead-generation problem.

Here are four theme categories you can create for your content calendar:

Aligning Content Formats With Goals

Lead Generation—How do I attract a potential new buyer to become part of our pipeline?

Brand Awareness—How do I spark any interest with a non-customer so they'll pay attention?

Brand Affinity—How do I get a buyer to experience our world? How can I get that buyer to have an emotional reaction to our brand?

Lead Nurturing—How do I stay top of mind for buyers in our pipeline who just aren't ready to buy?

The categories are also going to serve a purpose when you begin conducting deeper trend analysis to develop prescriptive improvements to your process. You'll want to validate that the insights you're building for an assumed buyer's journey stage is actually when he or she prefers to consume those insights. I can tell you that here at Sales for Life, we shocked ourselves when we did this analysis. We recognized quickly that infographics had become an incredible lead-nurturing tool for us, beyond the original brand-awareness design. Buyers were consuming up to five infographics all along their buying journey before purchasing our solution. We realized that as part of our blog creation mixture, we could begin allocating resources away from video blogging to infographic-based blogs. Both blog types were consuming approximately the same man-hours in production time, but the infographics were much more consumable for our buyers during the *how* stage of their buying journey. We are now spending the same man-hours to yield a far greater result.

"TURKEY SLICE" YOUR CORE CONTENT

In his book *Welcome to the Funnel*, Jason Miller talks about "turkey slicing," which, for any marketer keen to maximize volume and velocity, becomes a revelation.[1] I know Hubspot also does this exceptionally well. You create a large centralized insight that can spin off multiple smaller insights from its vast amount of content. For both InsideSales.com and Sales for Life, this vast amount of content starts with a webinar or virtual summit.

---

[1] Miller, Jason, *Welcome to the Funnel: Proven Tactics to Turn Your Social Media and Content Marketing up to 11,* Heavy Metal Thunder, 2014. http://www.welcometothefunnel.com/

Core Content Marketing Strategy

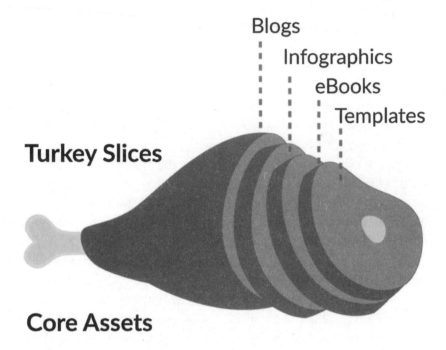

Blogs

Infographics

eBooks

Templates

Turkey Slices

Core Assets

From this single webinar, the video recording can be transcribed from video to text. That text can be leveraged for:

4 blogs
1 ebook
2 infographics (based on the quotes and facts in the video)

You can create a month's worth of insights from one event. As a secondary value, if you align these insights to interconnect to each other via calls to action and landing pages, you start creating a search engine optimization (SEO) monster. Unlike most insights, which are typically consumed in a silo, the leveraged materials shoot off from the primary asset. As a whole, you begin driving greater awareness to the topic, and your multitude of insights drives your brand higher and higher up the SEO food chain. Owning a topic on Google, regardless of how small a subcategory it is today, can pay dividends in the future. InsideSales.com did this twice, with *inside sales* and *sales acceleration.* At Sales for Life, we work diligently to own *social selling*, which is a fractional search term within a much larger sales training category. Subcategories such as digital sales, digital transformation, and sales and marketing integration are small search terms today, but we can monopolize these terms as they grow using the core content marketing strategy. Attack a keyword like a locust and devour that keyword until you own the crop, then move to the next plot of land.

TEMPLATES: LIKE PUNCHING OUT CAKES

I'm not diminishing the artistic side of digital marketing. Not at all. Our digital team has an incredible eye and flair for design. But do you know why my team gets to experiment? Because they've increased velocity so much. By saving hundreds of man-hours, they have time to experiment.

Think like you own a bakery. Of course, you want to build the coolest, tastiest, towering cake. But that's not your primary goal. Your goal is to build cakes to meet customer demand. A baker thinks about flair because he or she only needs to build one cake. A bakery creates a template for a cake so it can create units at scale. While it's not sexy, it keeps the doors to the bakery open.

With this same analogy, you need to create a template for everything—blogs, ebooks, videos, infographics—and slot insights into your designed templates. This saves your team the mental struggles of asking, "What should this look like?" You can also set your watch to each insight's development time, making everything highly predictable. At the time of this publication, our marketing team of five people, powered by our Insights Committee, average the following volume over a 30-day period:

50 blogs
2 ebooks
3 infographics
2 webinars

This is only possible when you have templates that allow you to punch out cakes within hours, not weeks.

ASSIGN TAGS FOR EACH INSIGHT BEFORE DEVELOPMENT

At first, your Insights Committee begins fueling new ad hoc ideas, which are typically gaps in your asset coverage. Over a period of time, powered by trend analysis (which we cover in Chapter 18), your marketing team drives the new insights that are created by the committee. Your team is then able to compare new content consumption data against your asset inventory to ensure you have the necessary balance in:

1. Themes
2. Buyer personas
3. Buyer's journey stage
4. Calls to action

Your team begins developing insights with a purpose! That's the best way I can describe it. You shift from an environment for extracting insights based on a sales professionals' interest *du jour* and instead adopt a more objective (while still collaborative) conversation with your Insights Committee about insights that will fuel your collective team's objectives.

FACTS AND DATA ARE THE CENTER OF THE STORY

After you have your insights idea and are ready to fit it inside your production template, fill the meat of the story with facts and data. Your sales professionals need this empirical evidence to fuel sales conversations. If possible, have one of your team members wield the dragnet for new analyst studies, reports, tests, and so on. Whatever the insights you're building, the value of the insight is centered around validation, contradicting, and expanding on data that shapes how your buyer thinks. These data points will be the first place your sales professionals kick off their conversation with a buyer.

CREATE A NEVER-ENDING STORY

Failing to create a never-ending story is easily one of the single largest pitfalls for digital marketing teams, and it is so easy to avoid. Marketing teams miss the basics of social selling. Social insights are consumed primarily in a silo, where a buyer reads a blog on LinkedIn or is invited via Twitter to an upcoming webinar. The buyer wasn't part of your nurture track, and even if he or she were, didn't notice 50 percent of the previous blogs that were emailed. The buyer then consumes a single insight, is generally intrigued, and shifts his or her priorities to learn more, but you've left the buyer with no direction to do so! That blog your sales professional shared had no next step, or the call to action was so subtle that even the buyer didn't catch it. This is also why sales professionals haven't naturally been supporters of content sharing or employee advocacy tools for content engagement: because they don't see buyers coming back for more! In Social Selling Mastery, we teach sales professionals to *never leave a naked message*! I beg you to *never end the story*. Great digital marketing teams know that insights will be consumed in a silo, thus we need to drive a buyer forward. Forward might mean from a blog talking about the *why* to driving a call-to-action to an ebook describing the *how*. Or, that story can be lateral, where an infographic on Topic ABC can be further expanded in a video as the call-to-action. There are two directions your never-ending story will lead a buyer:

1. **Forward,** walking the buyer in a linear progression from *why* to *how* to *who*.
2. **Laterally** within a buyer's journey stage. Think about a spin cycle within a particular stage. The buyer isn't ready to move forward, but he or she is interested in doing deeper learning.

When a buyer is consuming a blog, he or she must *always* have an option to move forward or laterally. The story never ends! So many of your buyers will enter a period called the *dead zone*, which is the dark, ill-communicative period of time when they're not consuming insights or speaking to your sales team. Digital content marketers need to leverage previous buyer trends and historical patterns to help the sales team overcome the *dead zone* and reignite the conversation. If a buyer falls off your radar because there is no logical call to action, and not enough brand awareness has been created upfront, that buyer may never find you again.

FUEL INSIGHTS DEVELOPMENT WITH "WINDOW TIME"

Window time is the downtime a sales professional has, which is predominately spent in the car, train, and airports. Instead of staring out the window, this is a great time for them to have phone interviews with the Insights Committee to uncover new ideas. If you record the call, you can use digital tools to convert it from audio to text. Your Insights Committee can talk a blog through in 5–10 minutes. Your marketing team can then pass the raw word document to a copy editor to clean up the story. Immediately, you have changed the velocity of your blog production forever! The scale of your blog development is now only limited by the number of phone calls you record or the speed at which your copy editor can clean up the stories. When we started *window time* at Sales for Life, we were able to double blog creation overnight. We then immediately deployed these blogs into the market with a cadence of one blog published per day; the ROI was staggering. Within 90 days, we had accelerated our new subscriber growth (new contacts subscribing to our blog) by 300 percent. The costs of window time were low. We had to pay for only speech-to-text software and a contract copy editor, but we were growing leads 300 percent faster!

CHAPTER 16

Organize Internal Content for Easy Access by Your Sales Force

If you can't explain it to a six year old, you don't understand it yourself.

—Albert Einstein

All the foundational work we did in Chapter 15 leads to the simplicity of designing your content library for sales professionals. I can't stress this enough: Keep it simple. You may already have a content library or three, depending on your company's size, but that doesn't mean they're effective. In fact, in most organizations we consult, the content library looks like an old, dusty filing cabinet in some remote bomb bunker, stuffed with details of the Cold War. I know your digital library can't literally get dusty, but you know in your heart if your sales professionals are leveraging the library as a pillar sales stack tool. When I mean pillar, I mean it's open every day with the other pillar tools: CRM, email, Google, LinkedIn.

I'm not being facetious. At Sales for Life, our resource library (which is both a client-facing and internal library for sharing insights with a buyer, available at www.salesforlife.com/resources) is used many times a day per sales professional.

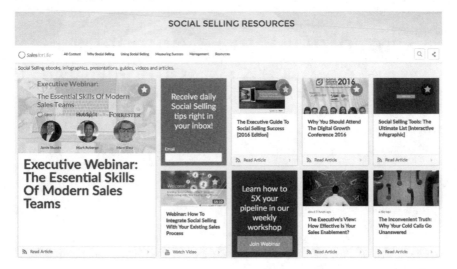

We believe our library is the definitive cataloging system for the world's best social selling information. Back to our intellectual property analogy with insights, we really do see our resource library as intellectual property. If a company copies our insights, it is like stealing a patent. That's how valuable we consider our insights to be. That's how I want you to reframe the value of your content library for your sales team.

STARTING YOUR CONTENT ORGANIZATIONAL SYSTEM

To fuel the *educate* section of Social Selling Mastery for sales professionals, we can't allow the team to rely on third-party tools to aggregate its favorite insights. In a best-case scenario, you will have chaotic insight sharing from sales and, in the worst case, the sales team doesn't share and your company is headed toward obscurity. If your mind is starting to wander beyond the library toward mechanizing an employee advocacy program (which we cover in this chapter)—*don't!* Employee advocacy tools are *not* a substitute for a rich library that allows sales professionals to find a very specific insight, for a very specific buyer, at a very specific time in that buyer's journey.

Employee advocacy tools, while highly effective if used properly, are a one-to-many program that are not best used for content organization. I've yet to see an employee advocacy tool organized with such tagging detail that it can stand in for a content library.

STEP 1: AUDIT SALES' ABILITY TO FIND YOUR INTERNAL LIBRARY

Assuming you have an existing content library, I want you to audit this properly. Don't guess. Don't assume. Naturally, marketing teams get very defensive about this topic because a content library is their initiative that has been months in the making, and they hate getting egg on their face if it's revealed the tool is not being used. But not you; you're not afraid! You're seeking to be world-class and are willing to put yourself on the line so that you may improve.

When I mean finding your internal content library, I mean it in the literal sense. Go to their desks, use a remote screen-sharing tool, and do whatever you need, but interview sales professionals and ask "Can you please grab an ebook from our internal content library?" I promise you, this is going to shock you! You may have preached this on every conference call for the last three months, but the results are still going to shock you. As an aside story, at nearly every speaking engagement I've done over the last two years, I'll ask the sales force I'm training to raise their hand if they've been on their respective corporate blog site before. On average, 33 percent of the sales professionals in that room have *never* been to their corporate blog site. Literally, they wouldn't even know where the web page is. Your first step is simple. Is your content lbrary located in a place that's very intuitive for a sales professional and will minimize their efforts to seek out this library?

STEP 2: AUDIT SALES' ABILITY TO NAVIGATE YOUR INTERNAL LIBRARY

Using the same sales professionals, ask them to find your insights in a scenario-based role play. *Don't* help them or lead them with tips or take over their mouse to navigate. Your content library is being used by sales professionals in different cities, states, or even countries, and you're not there to look over their shoulders. As an example of a scenario-based roleplay, you could ask:

> You have just finished a meeting with Jennifer, the CFO of Company ABC, and she mentioned that there could be a concern about financing operational projects over multiple years. When you get back to the office, you wanted to share with her an ebook that talks about the best practices for companies to extend projects over multiple years to mitigate cash flow concerns.

Take note of the sales professional's reaction in the first 10 seconds. This makes or breaks the effectiveness of the content library. If the sales professional is uncertain where to start or would need to spend more than five minutes finding a particular insight, the library has lost its effectiveness. Your buyers are asking dynamic questions. Shouldn't your content library also be dynamic?

STEP 3: REDESIGN THE FRAMEWORK OF YOUR CONTENT LIBRARY USING YOUR CONTENT CALENDAR TAGS

All of the logic that you placed in your content calendar is now coming back full swing to be placed into your content library. This is the level of granularity that your sales professionals need to find a very specific insight, for a very specific buyer, at a very specific time in that buyer's journey.

If you're part of a large organization with a multitude of business units and solutions, you may want to start the search criteria with the following logic. Sales professionals will still naturally gravitate toward product-based logic, so don't fight it. The logic you really want your content library to have is:

1. Sort by buyer journey stage: *why, how, when.*
2. Sort by buyer persona

Matching Insights With A Buyers Journey

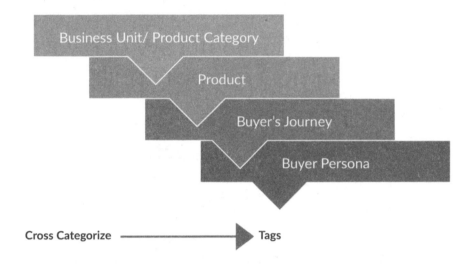

A dynamic content library should only present a sales professional the insights that match the desired search criteria. Rather than showcasing all 500 insights in the library, after a sales professional has selected a product category (or perhaps a tag for "Problems to be solved"), buyer's journey stage, and their targeted buyer persona, there might be 10 insights. These insights are then cross-tagged with keywords for search and tagged by asset type. Of the 10 insights available, there are 5 blogs, 2 ebooks, 2 videos, and 1 infographic. Now the sales professional can use his or her best judgment, based on the scenario, to share a very specific insight, for that very specific buyer, right now, because he knows where in the buying journey that buyer is.

STEP 4: TAGS FOR KEYWORD INDEXING

Buyers are dynamic. Sales is dynamic. Sales professionals need to be able to think on their feet. One of the challenges of static content libraries is that the title of an insight just doesn't provide enough context about the subject matter within the insight. It's also unrealistic to think your sales team will have read every single insight within the library.

Make your content library searchable. Start with the tagging system from your content calendar:

- By author
- By buyer journey stage
- By buyer persona

Create subfolder tags that are sales-centric. Don't make up tags and then gain the sales team's input later... ask them now! For example, Sales for Life uses dozens of tags like sales training, Twitter, LinkedIn, analytics, content marketing, and others.

STEP 5: LEVERAGE A VISUAL USER-INTERFACE TO HELP CONTEXTUALIZE THE INSIGHTS FOR SALES

As you improve your keyword indexing and think through the visual user interface (UI) from the sales professionals' perspective, you may want to think about what platform best suits those needs. Many companies start with simple intranet systems such as SharePoint, but realize that sales professionals are visual, just like your buyers. Marketing starts exploring tools that showcase image thumbnails and further graphic information about each insight. These same tools can also provide gamification and analytics around usage and engagement. An example of this tool is Uberflip (which Sales for Life uses).

ACCELERATING INSIGHTS WITH EMPLOYEE ADVOCACY

This is where many marketing teams mistake what a social selling program looks like by investing in an employee advocacy tool as a substitute for training, coaching, and behavioral change. As you saw in the *educate* and *engage* steps in Part Two, insight sharing is an essential *part* of social selling.

Step 1: Is Employee Advocacy Right for Us?

Employee advocacy is right for your team when insights distribution at scale has become a major challenge. Unfortunately, while you *think* that's your core issue, there are actually a variety of issues:

- Your team doesn't create enough fresh insights to fuel the tool to the point of keeping the sales team engaged.
- The insights you create aren't insights; they're glorified press releases and product information.

I've seen the inside of approximately 50 companies' employee advocacy tools over the last two years. In most instances, they are violating both of these issues. The company just doesn't create new insights fast enough and the insights it does create have headlines like "Company ABC launches XYZ Product." Who gives a damn! Your buyer doesn't.

Think long and hard before you think employee advocacy is going to be the miracle drug for your insight-sharing machine.

Step 2: Implementation Best Practices

The results of an effective employee advocacy program are enormous. Imagine having hundreds or thousands of voices in the market, all working in unison. This is possible if you execute a program with the right intentions and the sales team, company wide, is generally excited for the platform.

1. Interview the sales team on what insights they read. Which internal insights do they feel have added the most value and what third-party insights do they gravitate toward?
2. Interview your buyers on which insights they read for the same reasons as above.
3. Schedule regular additions to insights. Your Insights Factory has to be consistent. If the insights are being updated ad hoc, your sales

team will begin to question the difference between this tool and your content library. Employee advocacy tools specialize in timely content, which can help you highlight an event or campaign.

4. Organize the tool with the same tags and structure as your content library. The tool needs to be searchable in the same way a library is. These tools are typically able to provide you with analytics on which insights are most used, which your content library might not be able to do.

5. Measure everything and gamify. Sync your tool to your marketing automation using tracking codes to ensure you understand buyer consumption for future trend analysis. Sales professionals are also used to being in competition, so they gamify the process. We stack-rank our team by buyers' engagement.

CHAPTER 17

Discover Inbound and Outbound Marketing Hacks to Accelerate Lead Velocity

I can't understand why people are frightened of new ideas. I'm frightened of the old ones.

—John Cage

Discovery is where the good marketing teams are left behind by the great ones. Corporate marketing campaigns do an excellent job of nurturing existing buyers in their pipeline but they often lack innovative ingredients to grow a new pipeline. Think about it. They share insights through their corporate LinkedIn, Twitter, Facebook, and corporate email accounts, which helps educate existing leads but only slightly attracts new leads. Remember from our exercise in Chapter 14, we're responsible for a big lift that will help our sales team meet and exceed their sales quota.

As a digital marketing team, there are dozens of paid, earned, owned, and shared media ideas that you can execute. This is not a book about general content marketing principles. This is a book about hacking innovative digital content ideas that fuel social selling—ideas that have been proven successful and that you're most likely not doing today.

TACTIC 1: OPERATION LAND GRAB

In Chapter 15, we helped you accelerate your blog development volume with an Insights Committee and shrink production velocity using "Window Time." These simple but effective blog accelerators could allow your blogs to be published from once a week to once a day and beyond. Your company is now becoming a beacon of intellectual property, and companies that share your industry space are keen to leverage your intellectual property machine as a guest blogger. There will be very few companies in your industry that can supply themselves with enough great insights and will seek external guest contributors. Progressive marketers at these companies will also recognize the power of third-party thought leadership on their blog to provide greater credibility.

Operation Land Grab is like a trip into the Wild West. During the Gold Rush, prospectors raced westward to stake a claim to new land. These prospectors captured new land for free by putting in hard work, time, and effort rather than money. Using this analogy, there are companies in your industry (e.g., consulting services, technology products, industry analysts, etc.) that have the land (i.e., new leads *not* in your pipeline) that your sales team wants to attract. All you need to do is capture this land. Using your high volume of insights, you will develop a scheduled system to guest blog on the companies' websites that will drive their database of leads into your sales pipeline. How does this work?

a. Develop a list of potential lead owners (companies and their websites).
b. Contact these lead owners about their guest blogging schedules.
c. Create a content calendar just for Operation Land Grab.
d. Communicate the calendar and new volume demands to the Insights Committee.
e. Keep the Insights Committee on schedule to create these guest blogs
f. Ensure every guest blog has your call to action back to *your* lead capturing insight (such as an ebook).

I can't stress the last part enough. Remember that insights, like blogs, are consumed in a silo. You must drive their leads into your marketing automation system! Sales for Life has more than 30 guest-blogging partners at the time of this publication. We had set a goal to guest blog every business day so that we had a third-party blog post published somewhere in the world each business day. We found that while we have more than 30 partners, five or so will drive 80 percent of the lead flow. With no surprise, these are the largest publications that have hundreds of thousands, even millions, of readers. That doesn't mean we would abandon the small company blog. Remember, if that website attracted one lead, and that one lead was hyper-qualified and became a buyer, that cost-of-customer acquisition would still be very, very cheap.

TACTIC 2: EVENT LEAD EXCHANGES

Webinars and virtual summits have been an incredible lead-generation source for our business. The secret sauce: It's not really about the content in the webinar. Of course, the webinar needs to be compelling, but the real value of a webinar is massive acceleration of new leads. This is accomplished by inviting guest panelists and promotional partners into the event. The panelist will be part of the presentation during the event and he or she will be responsible for promoting the event just like you will. If you've chosen your panelists correctly, they will provide high-octane volumes of net new leads into your system. But often forgotten are the promotional partners for your event. They are similar to sponsors, except rather than exchanging money, you will exchange leads.

As a best practice, we build promotional packages for our panelist and promotional partners that outline social post schedules, email templates, and so on. Within that promotional package, we outline the ideal customer profile (ICP) that we'd like to attract for the event. Clarity is key! What is the size, industry, and region that our promotional partner needs to fuel new leads. We then strike a deal with that partner on an exchange, starting at 1:1, and accelerating to 5:1 for virtual summits where there are thousands of leads created. For every new lead a promotional partner places into your CRM, you'll populate their CRM with an equally valuable lead that they don't currently have. This is the ultimate form of co-opetition. All of a sudden, for larger webinars and virtual summits, you're adding hundreds or perhaps thousands of new ideal buyers into your CRM to begin the nurturing process. Within weeks or months, those ICPs will consume your insights, and a portion will develop into marketing or sales-qualified leads. This is the ultimate fishing with a net to provide fuel for your sales development representatives (SDRs) to qualify new leads.

TACTIC 3: REPURPOSE AND RECYCLE YOUR TOP 10 PERCENT

Hubspot, a leading marketing automation platform and a company I believe is always on the forefront of digital content marketing, has some incredible analytics from its own blog: "92% of their leads come from blog posts over 30 days old. 30 blog posts (0.5% of their blog database) represents 46% of all their leads!"[1]

That doesn't mean you can abandon creating a high volume of new insights. You need to first achieve search engine optimization (SEO) power over your competitors. Next, you need enough data points to understand which insights are your best performers. Once you've established this baseline, you'll quickly recognize the Pareto Law within your own insights—80 percent of their consumption and conversion will come from 20 percent of the insights. But which insights are the productive ones?

Scaling Social Selling Mastery is about shrinking the velocity required to create a new asset, so the time-management game starts to work in your favor. This is why we love to repurpose and recycle techniques. The most important value to repurpose and recycle is that

---

[1] September 16, 2015, http://www.inboundmarketingagents.com/inbound -marketing-agents-blog/bid/364451/INBOUND-Insights-Use-Old-Blog-Posts -to-Generate-New-Leads

you're not starting the SEO clock from 0, as your top assets already have hundreds or thousands of views. These assets have become key educational pieces for your buyers, and your sales team likes sharing them. Now, you're only going to build on the SEO value that's been established, perhaps helping this insight rank number one on Google.

Here are steps you can follow to help accelerate your repurpose-and-recycle system:

1. Identify the top blogs, ebooks, infographics, and so on based on SEO (traffic, clicks, conversion).
2. Run the copy through Google Analytics for keywords. Can you spike the SEO by adding new keywords that are hot in your market?
3. Cut the insight and paste it into your new insights template. Are there key ingredients missing, like a call to action or bold H1 headlines that perform better in Google?
4. Add updated statistics, stories, images, and metadata to refresh the insight.
5. Change the call to action to drive to a new and better performing next step.
6. Adjust the insight's date of publication to reflect today's date.

The last step is a lesson in psychology. Both your buyers and your sales team will gravitate toward the new. When you do a Google search, how much does the publish date play into your clicking? We as consumers always want the latest information. By adjusting the date of publication for this article, you'll have sales professionals begin leveraging the insight because it's fresh, *and* you'll have the loyalist sales professionals who use the insight because it's effective.

At Sales for Life, we're refreshing our top 10 percent performing insights every quarter. Our team gathers the data and ensures we're polishing a mixture of:

1. Top performers by eyeballs (clicks and shares). This helps with brand awareness.
2. Top performers by conversion, focusing on lead generation.

3. Make sure we're polishing a mixture of asset types, and not allowing specific types like ebooks to grow too stale.

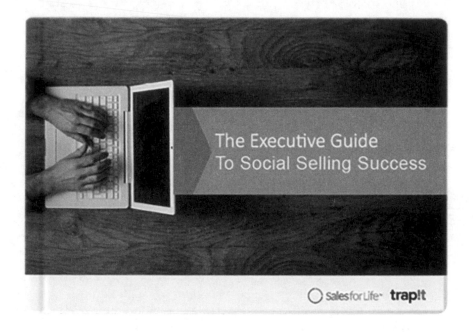

CHAPTER 18

Evaluate Your Customer's Journey

Find the Trends and Improve Key Sales Interactions

Human behavior flows from three main sources: desire, emotion, and knowledge.

—Plato

To begin fishing with a spear, your marketing team will need to understand the desire, emotion, and accumulated knowledge that your buyers are providing. You will map their digital fingerprints to gain a full picture of their content-consumption story. Account-based marketing efforts are only as effective as the trends and analysis you've done on your buyers. I believe that the information you learn in this chapter is typically the most underutilized but powerful way your team is going to help sales meet quota attainment. Crush your competition by understanding thy buyer!

WHAT IS THE CONTENT-CONSUMPTION STORY?

The content-consumption story is a road map of the digital fingerprints that your buyer has left on all your insights. Go beyond your blog and look for your buyer on your website, emails, social networks, and so on. That buyer is arming him- or herself with information to make informed decisions, but also leaving a set of clues for you to follow. These clues can be mapped to help you understand the volume, velocity, and probability patterns you need to scale. If you extrapolate enough customer data, you can then develop a trending story. These trends help you make prescriptive improvements to your process.

GO BEYOND LEAD SOURCING: START EMPIRICALLY PROVING LEAD INFLUENCE

At this point, we're putting down the fishing net and, before picking up our spears, we're looking at some sonar equipment to understand fishing patterns. To this point in our insights factory, we've applied great tactics to accelerate lead flow that will help fuel new sales conversations. But the sales team needs more than just nets and nets of fish. They need to know that for each fish (or whale for that matter) they've been following, you in marketing have been placing tracking devices on the fish. Your sales team will work a buyer and the buying committee within an account for weeks, months, and even years. The blind spot that we talked about in Chapter 13 will hinder your sales team's progression if there is no tracking device. A tracking device does your sales team no good if the professionals can't look into the sonar equipment in real time. You need to help your sales team to understand the content consumption patterns of previous buyers to help them contextualize its experiences with its currently engaged buyers.

Every single day, your buyers are learning from someone. They might be learning on your website, and they might be reading your latest ebook right now. This is all part of lead influence. While the lead may have come into your sales team's hands months ago from another source, it is formulating a buying plan because of the contributions from both sales *and* marketing. If you look at our clients, basically 100 percent of them are influenced by marketing efforts, as they're consuming seven to eight insights before they buy. Sales is doing its part by having various on- and offline conversations with our buyer, and marketing is doing its part to educate the buyer online, behind the scenes, when sales isn't directly talking to that buyer.

HOW CAN TECHNOLOGY PLAY A HUGE ROLE?

If you want to remove the blind spots from sales, get marketing automation data in the professionals' hands in real time, directly tied into their customer relationship manager (CRM) instance. That means that a sales professional can see what a buyer is consuming right now, and search the buyer's history for what he or she has not consumed. Both Marketo and Eloqua have profiler tools to present this information to a sales professional in real time within an I-frame in Salesforce.com. At Sales for Life, we use Hubspot, with a browser extension called Sidekick. I can monitor the real-time content consumption of any assigned buyer through both an I-Frame within Salesforce.com or as a pop-up trigger alert in Google Chrome. Do you want to change your sales team's perceived value of what insights are doing for your buyers? Nothing is more powerful than sales executives realizing that one of their top prospective accounts is reading your company's ebook right now—oh, and just read your newest blog five minutes before that. Wait . . . they're on your solutions page now. Alert your sales executive! It's time to pick up the phone!

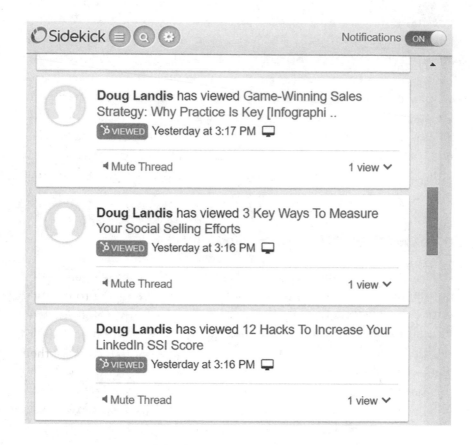

WHAT ARE THE STEPS TO CAPTURING A BUYER'S CONTENT-CONSUMPTION STORY?

Step 1: Choose One Customer to Analyze

I recommend that you select one customer success story. Don't boil the ocean. Work with the sales team to identify a customer who presented multiple challenges, perhaps did some stopping and starting in his or her process, but also is reflective of a typical deal. Chop out the anomalies of bluebirds who swooped into the CRM and closed within 10 days. They just won't provide you an accurate picture of your typical buyer. In preparation for your customer analysis, you'll need the following:

1. Marketing automation history
2. CRM history
3. The sales professional(s) who worked the account to help fill in any missing information

The sales professional is critical because, let's face it, not every sales interaction will have been properly placed into the CRM. You'll need the sales professional(s) involved in this deal to show emails, phone-call summaries, notes, and so on for any interaction that isn't clear in the CRM.

Using a spreadsheet, plot your buyer's journey across rows and, in the next row below, fill in the details of your typical sales process across the spreadsheet. I recommend that the buyer's journey and sales process be in rows 1 and 2 so your sales professionals get a clear understanding of the chronological timeline you're trying to capture. When we've done this exercise internally, our buyer's journey in columns 1, 2, and 3 are named "Why," "How," and "Who," early, middle, and late stages of the journey. Sales professionals can plot their sales process (i.e., first call, discovery, consensus-building call, demo, proposal, legal review) within this three-column sequence.

Begin plotting sales interactions first; voicemails, phone calls, emails—nothing is too small. Highlight the dates of these interactions. Plot these interactions from first touchpoint all the way until the close, so include discovery calls, demos, proposals, and so on. Next, plot the consumed insights and dates over the same timeline. Highlight marketing assets in a different color if you need to visually distinguish everything. Note the assets by type, dates between assets consumed, dates between assets consumed in proximity to a sales interaction. You should be left with a road map of everything that sales and marketing did to influence this won customer.

Step 2: Isolate a Single Observation

From this exercise, you may have a few observations. First, the sales professionals will have their mouths open, realizing that their buyer had been on your website reviewing various insights without informing the sales team. Hopefully, there is a nugget of gold to extract. This could be the proximity of content consumption 24 hours before or after a major sales interaction. Perhaps this buyer consumed a variety of asset types, but the headline and topic of these insights were basically the same. You now have a template to scale this process.

Step 3: Scale by Mapping Larger Pools of Clients

Now that you have the template for implementing this analysis, you'll want to map all your top customers. Depending on volume, you may start with recent transactions. However you choose to dissect this information, you need a sample size that is large enough to give you the comfort that the results will represent your entire client base.

Step 4: Regression Analysis to Isolate Trends

Now the fun begins. You will begin plotting client after client, giving you further knowledge about how your buyer is conducting his or her due diligence. As you begin analyzing the entire buyer story, segment consumption patterns into the three buyer's journey stages: why, how, who. You'll want to understand what's happening in great detail when a buyer is first discovering his or her problem (the *why*), then the patterns that are helping him or her progress.

Here are examples of trends you'll want to discover:

- How many insights, on average, is a buyer consuming? Is that similar for all buyer personas or size of customer?
- Within a buyer's total consumption, how much (as a percentage or number of assets) is consumed before the first sales interaction? Can you make a case for CEB's statistic that 57 percent of the buying journey is happening without sales?
- What is the percentage of consumption a buyer does when interacting in later stages with your sales executives? During

the how and who stages, how much are digital insights still influencing a buyer?

- At the asset-type level, are specific asset types dramatically outperforming others to create new leads? Are sales executives nurturing their accounts?
- Are specific asset types being consumed in high volume during a specific buyer's journey stage that you didn't anticipate?

You can slice and dice this data all day long. Remember, your main goal is to understand:

1. Volumes needed for future production.
2. Velocity needed to get assets into the market quicker.
3. Probability that an asset will convert.

Each of these three main metrics will be the focal point of your incremental improvements. As an example, when we ran this analysis among a portion of our client base, the following trends caught our eye:

- Our buyer is consuming 7.4 assets before buying.
- Forty-three percent of that consumption happens before our first sales conversation.
- Seventy-five percent of that consumption happens before our sales executives discuss our solution during a discovery call.
- Infographic-based blogs had five times the opportunity for greater production development. If you analyzed our production time against remaining production resources and cross-analyzed against an infographic's ROI, we can accelerate our production by five times before we hit a capacity issue.

Step 5: Arm Your Sales Team with This Information to Improve Sales Conversations

Imagine the power this information has in your sales team's hands. Your professionals know what insights should best be shared, to which buyers, and at what stages of that buyer's journey. They'll be able to better qualify a buyer if he or she is not consuming insights that meet the average consumption patterns of previous buyers. This content consumption minimum has been highly valuable for our sales team. If a buyer is not actively engaged in our insights, a red flag goes up and we ask ourselves, "How interested is this buyer in our solution?" This saves countless hours to ensure our sales team isn't spinning its wheels.

The communication of these trends needs to extend beyond your Insights Committee. This data will enable your entire team to see a system that allows for better spear fishing.

6. Create a Prescriptive Process to Making Incremental Improvements

This year, I decided I would write down my current weight on January 1 and then I gave myself a goal for December 31. But as an extra step, I also then framed the goal and placed it on my work desk. Remember that my lagging indicator for the Jamie Shanks Weight-Loss Challenge is my weight on December 31. If I don't hit that goal, I can't do anything about it on New Year's Eve. I need to be looking at my current indicators: What is my weight today; if I lost X pounds per month or quarter, could I hit my goal?

It's time to dust off your initial production capacity results from Chapter 14 and begin to develop a plan for testing ways to slightly improve volumes, velocity, and probability in each campaign, in each month. Here are examples of ways you can think about making incremental improvements. Remember, don't just click your fingers and decide on smallish ways to improve. These improvements, done month over month, have to align to the goals set out for meeting sales quotas.

Volume:

- What can we do next month to double our blog volume?
- Can we shift resources to improve volumes on high performing assets? Can we outsource a contractor to accelerate things?
- Can we ask each Insights Committee member to tell two blog stories (rather than one this month), so we can double our blog output?

- As we build the "8 steps to XYZ ebook," can we also carve out the eight headlines to make eight, 60-second video blogs for next month?

Velocity

- What can we do next month to shorten our production time on webinars by 33 percent?
- Can we ask our panelist if we can just be the moderator, and he or she the subject matter expert? Can they then supply the presentation deck? Can we use the promotional package and schedule from last month's webinar and get these panelists promoting the event quickly?
- Can we leverage the email copy from our top performing webinar and recycle its style for this upcoming webinar?

Probability

- What can we do to convert 50 percent more leads next month without dramatically changing our production volume, as the team is overcommitted on a few projects?
- Can we invite two panelists from Company ABC to be part of next month's webinar? Last time, the webinar drove 500 registrants and 20 new leads come from it.
- Can we get the sales team sharing the "XYZ infographic" heavily, as it's been the highest-converting asset in the last six months? That infographic created 10 leads just from our corporate account; we should get 50 new leads from our 100 sales professionals.
- Can we repurpose the ebook "The ROI of XYZ" and add quotes from the top 20 industry experts. If we get them socially sharing this ebook, it will drive at least 50 more leads.

Your team is experimenting, but experimenting with more and more information to become more scientific. It doesn't take long for your marketing efforts to become predictable. Whenever you can make your marketing efforts predictable, you can scale them. Work that predictable scale with your sales team to plot a course for meeting and exceeding their sales quota.

SCALING UP WITH SALES OPERATIONS AND SALES ENABLEMENT

How Do We Mitigate Skill Gaps with Our New Hires?

A chain is no stronger than its weakest link, and life after all is a chain.

—William James

I'd like you to imagine that you coach a sports team. You've been hired after the annual draft and need to start assembling your final roster during training camp. How do you think the most successful coaches would approach training camp?

1. Push only last year's roster to tackle new advanced plays.
2. Make sure that their newly drafted teammates can master the basic plays that the entire team has always executed.

I hope the answer seems obvious in sports. But why doesn't this seem obvious in a sales and marketing department? This is where you can help shape your annual sales kick-off (SKO) and quarterly business reviews (QBRs) to incorporate skill-based training. It's been my observation that most SKOs and QBRs are far too product-training heavy. I'll meet streams of newly hired sales professionals at these events and pick their brains about their onboarding process. The process was a firehouse of information about how to sell the product. Unfortunately, these newly hired sales professionals are missing the basic blocking and tackling of your core team's sales methodology, let alone adding new skills such as social selling. This is how random acts of social can metastasize in your business. Before you know it, there is a huge discrepancy between how a 10-year veteran and your new sales professionals are selling. Compound this by having hundreds of sales professionals in different regions and countries, constantly prioritizing new campaigns, and stopping and starting new initiatives. We're talking about utter chaos. This chaos has two negative business outcomes for sales organizations striving to hit sales quota.

1. They'll have a much more difficult time helping each sales professional meet his or her sales quota if everyone is selling differently.
2. When they roll out initiatives to some sales professionals and not others, the prioritization of needs for each sales professional becomes almost too dynamic. This results is not one skill gap, but many. How can you measure the effectiveness of your sales force if there isn't an even a baseline to measure everyone against?

You as a sales enablement leader need to change your new hire program to align all skills shared by every sales professional. The knowledge your top sales professionals have and execute on each day needs to be the same as what's in the playbook you hand your new hires. We've seen companies recognize that changing a sales culture works exactly like a sports team. Strong sports franchises that have down years or cultural challenges will fix their problems with new players from the draft. These sports franchises know that the most successful teams will grow organically and develop a positive culture together. Player by player, the old culture is pushed out by the new culture. If you're keen to develop a synergistic ecosystem, I highly recommend you incorporate social selling directly into the new-hire program. In this approach, companies use the first week of onboarding to tackle the company's fundamentals such as culture and product training. Immediately after that, the sales enablement team will begin rolling out skill-based training to ensure every sales professional is selling the same way. *Don't wait!* I've seen companies that didn't even have proper territory assignments and compensation plans ready for new-hire training. Can you really afford to have a sales professional executing in market for three months, without the same playbook as your other team members?

I'm a huge fan of role-based training and practicums to test that a newly learned skill is translating into a sales outcome. Within the Social Selling Mastery program, we test each sales professional with a real-life scenario in which the sales professional must create a net new opportunity based on their social selling skills. What inspired this practicum (beyond the fact that practice is known to improve recall) is what Hubspot does with its new hires. Hubspot sells its marketing automation solution to marketers and the company wants its newly hired sales professionals to empathize with marketers. To accomplish this, each new hire is responsible for building a personal website and promoting the website using content, paid advertisements, and so on. There is a defined goal for each website, which is to teach each sales professional the difficulties that marketers have in gaining high rankings on Google.

Using this same logic, I recommend your new hires sit with the digital content marketing team for a period of time. Watch the team create, organize, distribute, and evaluate its campaigns. Have the team see exactly how a marketer supports the sales team's success. Have the sales team start at the foundation by learning the buyer's journey. You can't afford to have these sales professionals cycle into their sales role and slip into the same myopic view that most sales professionals have, especially the seasoned veterans. As the old saying goes: Just because you sell hammers doesn't mean everything is a nail. Broaden your new hire's appreciation for sales and marketing integration, and the power of Team Revenue.

CHAPTER 20

Ongoing Coaching

How Do We Create a Repeatable Process?

I am still learning.

—Michelangelo at age 87

REINFORCE ACTION

One of the hardest business routines for me to break was checking my email when I first got up in the morning. Email is such a time suck! But I couldn't help myself. I actually was cognizant of the fact that I was having a chemical reaction in my brain that made me feel like I had missed something if I didn't check my emails. It wasn't until about two years ago that I made a shift. The inception started with a simple quote I came across, but I can't remember where. The quote is: "Emails are other people's priorities, not yours." With that simple quote, and countless other lessons from people such as Tim Ferriss, I decided to change. My first change was to replace the email checking action with an insights checking action on Feed.ly. I would spend 5–10 minutes reading a few articles, some for self-interest and some to be shared with buyers. I would then share an insight to my LinkedIn and Twitter network before really starting my day. That was it. That was one step among other social selling steps that helped build my company. Instead of nose-diving into emails that would consume my time and alter my daily priorities, I would first serve my brain and my buyer with insights. Over time, I later evolved so my email checking routine meant I hit the inbox only three times per day:

7:30–8:30~AM: Scan for customer emails, and make those a priority. Then clean out the inbox.

12:00–12:30~PM: Only answer customer emails or anything that seems urgent.

8:00–10:00~PM: While working on the couch with my wife, clean out my email inbox.

This routine has made me exponentially more efficient during business hours. I now spend my day helping my team and serving my customers, instead of focusing on nonessential tasks that others would like to inject into my daily priorities.

Was this difficult to change? Yes.

Did this happen overnight? No.

My behavioral change required constant self-supervision and reinforcement of a new habit.

I bring up this analogy because it showcases that creating a Social Selling Mastery organization does not happen overnight either. In fact, hundreds of sales enablement leaders we've met have tried to kick start an internally designed social selling program, only to fail because they tackled the project like they had other skill-based training—in a half-day workshop. One-and-done training for sales professionals, for a topic as dynamic as social selling, is guaranteed to result in only 10 percent retention two weeks later. Do not develop a social selling program unless you're going to create checks and balances, gates and hurdles, for sales professionals to master before continuing their learning path. Social selling isn't like teaching a sales professional how to pick up a telephone receiver. Social selling has the same dynamics as teaching a new sales professional how to pick up the phone, dial, talk to a CFO, objection handle, book a discovery call, host that discovery call, and qualify the buyer for the sales team. Can you accomplish this in a half-day workshop? Workshops are the perfect environment to create buy-in and a groundswell of initial action within the sale force, but don't mistake it for world-class training and coaching.

HOW DO YOU CREATE A REINFORCEBLE TRAINING PROGRAM?

This is the problem that Sales for Life set out to solve. We cracked this code first for social selling, and it's allowed us to service more than 250 companies around the world. I consider it to be one of our secret sauces. We call it the Learning Loop, a cadence that repeats itself using various reinforcement mechanisms to help ensure adoption. We didn't wake up one day in 2012 and draw this Learning Loop on the walls of our office like cavemen. No, the Learning Loop is a stone, polished by what we have learned from customer after customer engagement. Here is how the Learning Loop works:

The loop has a cadence cycle of one week. Each week, we deliver new ideas and best practices to sales and marketing professionals using a variety of methods. Remember that everyone learns differently; in fact, 85 percent of your team will be visual learners, but many are also auditory or kinetic learners (learn by doing and practicum). The Learning Loop accounts for this variety of learning styles.

1. **Crowdsourced Curriculum:** While this doesn't mean much to you, this is how we scale Sales for Life's Social Selling Mastery program. We recognized that best practices were going to be developed around the world, not always by us. So we empowered the more than 60,000 students in our system to fuel new ideas and best practices in the curriculum to keep it organically growing. Within your organization, if you're designing your own social selling training program, it must evolve and grow. This isn't like a traditional sales methodology created 30 years ago. Social selling is fluid, and the tactics and best practices are changing monthly. You'll need to find a way to capture these new ideas so you can keep your sales force informed. Within the Learning Loop, our crowdsourcing mechanism is feeding new ideas and best practices (in the form of a module) to the sales and marketing professionals on a weekly basis.

2. **Instructor-Led Training:** Your sales and marketing team can participate in lunch-and-learn sessions during which best practices are contextualized and shown tactically to the team. These are scenario-based micro workshops, typically one hour long that show real-life application. They're live and instructor-led (Sales for Life uses virtual technology for global classroom scale) so the team can manipulate the scenarios based on their current needs.

3. **Learning Portal:** In this digital age, your team will need a mechanism to replay and reinforce the learnings from the instructor-led sessions. We developed a library of videos, guides, road maps, and templates that sales and marketing professionals can leverage as they self-pace learn. A learning management system (LMS) makes a perfect library, as it provides learning data for your leading indicators.

4. **Daily Coaching:** The most important vehicle for learning is one-on-one support. Your team will have real-time questions that need answering, and not everyone is comfortable interrupting an instructor-led session for their specific needs. We created a public open forum each day, for one hour, for sales and marketing professionals to ask questions about what-if scenarios, engagement best practices, and so on. You need to make a subject matter expert available to your team, as eLearning and live training just can't help everyone. Remember that you will have a curve of rock stars, core performers, and laggards. Don't let the core performers drift out of your program because they can't find a way to have their questions answered. I've found that disengagement in a training program stems from two sore spots:

   1. Camp A: "I don't believe this is valuable." That should be a red flag for long-term viability in your business.

   2. Camp B: "I had so many questions compounding week after week, that I got frustrated and tuned out."

      Tuning out is exactly like when we were in school. The students who tuned out were frustrated by how far behind they got and just gave up. Mitigate this from happening by developing an open forum to allow for highly customized coaching.

5. **ROI Measurements:** This is where your leading and current indicators become so vital. You need to know which students are showing great signs of adoption versus students who are falling behind. The struggling students should be encouraged to attend the upcoming daily coaching sessions. The students who are successfully adopting new practices can highlight what they're doing so you can shine a spotlight on their success at the following week's instructor-led session. Your indicators will keep you on track week after week and ensure you're not standing in a boardroom 90 days later, dumbfounded that you can't understand why the sales team doesn't seem to do what we asked. The warning signs and obvious reinforcement changes you need to make will be in front of you each week.

CHAPTER 21

How Do We Effectively Scale a Social Selling Program Company-Wide?

Growth is never by mere chance; it is the result of forces working together.

—James Cash Penney

AMPLIFY AND SCALE

Scaling a Social Selling Mastery program within your organization is going to require empirical evidence of success. Yes, of course, one business unit will take a leap of faith to become a guinea pig for a pilot. But without quantifiable results, this is where we see projects hit a major wall. Although we covered measuring social selling success in Chapter 5, we must help the sales operations and sales enablement team capture indicators. Based on the corporate goals set forth before you began, you will align your leading, current, and lagging indicators to capture data necessary to determine if you've accomplished your goals. The most popular system to leverage is the Kirkpatrick Model, known for its "5 Evaluation Levels of Training Measurement."

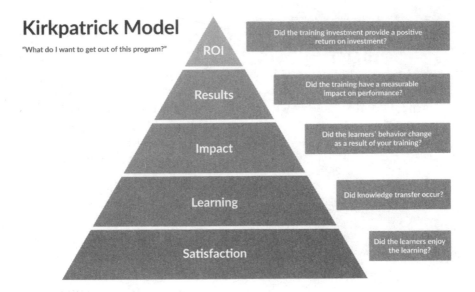

As I mentioned previously in the book, I often see sales enablement leaders focus their key performance indicators (KPIs) on the first level of the Kirkpatrick Model—satisfaction. These leaders measure the value of skill-based training using feedback surveys. While this information is valuable to shape future versions of a training program, it doesn't help determine if sales goals have been met.

Of course we want ROI data, but the realities and dynamics of training programs can sometimes make capturing the ultimate lagging indicator (sales pipeline and sales bookings) a long time horizon. I'll give you an example. You have a corporate mandate to scale a Social Selling Mastery program globally over the next 12 months. Here lies the problem: Your average sale is complex, with an average cycle of 9 to 18 months. To make this timeline, you need to be scaling the training program from Americas to Europe to Latin America to Asia every 90 days. While you'll have great data on leading indicators and trending current indicators that are showing promise, you just don't have hard ROI data yet! This is where you need to be capturing evidence within the five evaluation levels as your leading, current, and lagging indicator successes.

Level 1—Satisfaction: Think of this as post-training surveys. What was a sales professional's main takeaway? Rank this training against previous trainings.

Level 2—Learning: This is the data from your sales and marketing professionals' learning behavior. Did the team put in the effort to learn? Did they engage in class, complete the assignments, and review the supporting materials? I find that sales enablement leaders put a ton of stock in these metrics as their final lagging indicator, which is critical and proven to drive future predictable behavior. But you want to be world-class and seek to leverage this data for what it really is—a predictor of future success, not a measurement of final success.

Level 3—Application: This is the data from real-time sales and marketing execution in the field. Pulling together data from marketing automation, a customer relationship manager (CRM), employee advocacy, and LinkedIn Sales Navigator answers the question, "Are the sales professionals applying the knowledge and creating new sales activity?" Level 3 is where you start getting global C-level executives intrigued about social selling. They can see the sales team is executing, and they can assume that results are soon to follow. Without Level 3 application data, you're bound to get blank stares and skeptics. At that point you can expect to hear, "Come back to me when we have more evidence of success."

Level 4—Business Impact: In every customer engagement, we build a road map to capture Level 4 data during a pilot or Phase 1 rollout. We need data to provide a lagging indicator of goals that sales, marketing, and enablement establish at the onset of the project. Now, you're talking about scaling social selling to other regions, or business units armed with data on: increased sales pipeline, net new opportunities created, stories about penetrating top-strategic accounts, and the impact this deal will have on the business.

Level 5—Return on Investment (ROI): Don't believe that you can calculate this in 90 days or that it is as simple as looking at projected sales for 12 months. Calculating a true ROI requires two parts to the equation:

Costs

- Man-hours: Planning, building, training, coaching
- Investments: Tools, consultants, trainers
- Intangibles: Projects you couldn't launch because you were fully engaged in a social selling initiative

Gains

- Sales: 12–24 months of sales that have trailed into the business from social selling
- Sales-Quota Attainment: Percentage of sales professionals who met quota in Year 1 and Year 2 after a social selling initiative versus those percentages in previous years. Of course, other factors play into making sales quota, but this helps make a compelling case for social selling implementation.
- Employee Recruiting and Retention: As the market hears about your new sales environment, is it easier to attract and retain team members? Are they more engaged?

RETURNS

You're looking to justify a compelling case that shows a 10–20-time return on costs. For every $1 you spend on internal resources, tools, consultants, trainers and so on, did the organization make $10 to $20 in topline sales for the business? Did you change your market position in specific territories as a higher percentage of those sales professionals met or exceeded their targets?

For Sales for Life, we have built measuring levels of the Kirkpatrick Model in each of the three indicator stages. Each of the levels within the Kirkpatrick Model triangle is aligned in a progressive sequence. As an example, in Level 2, learning, the leading indicator to watch is LMS log-in information. Are students logging in each week or binge learning? How have students that learn in a consistent sequence performed historically against binge learners? Next, a current indicator for Level 2 is deeper learning behavior in the LMS. Do they watch only a portion of the e-learning curriculum, or the entire program? Finally, the lagging indicator for a Level 2 evaluation is certification. As we discussed in Chapter 5, we've proven that learning is a predictor to sales success. But we've also proven that partial learning isn't nearly as valuable as full certification. Our lagging indicator is to ensure everyone is certified, but we should be watching those Level 2 leading and current indicators week-by-week to meet our certification goals.

Indicators from Learning to Results

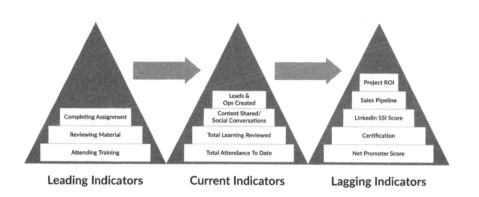

Leading Indicators	Current Indicators	Lagging Indicators

REAL-TIME DASHBOARDS FOR CURRENT AND LAGGING INDICATORS

Scaling your social selling project can't always wait for the next big boardroom presentation. Don't wait until 30 days after a social selling pilot to compile lagging indicators; if you do, you just waste valuable time. Have your tools provide real-time reports so you can be pushing the social selling agenda on a more routine basis. Just like learning anything new, people need to hear and see the story multiple times for it to resonate. Start building your use case for global scale today, not tomorrow.

Conclusion

As an entrepreneur, I feel blessed. When George Albert and I merged our businesses in February 2012, we set out to build a scalable organization. We knew we didn't want to be stuck in the consultant lifestyle-business trap. We had aspirations of global engagements. I didn't know at the time of our merger, probably because we were both broke, that we would grow a company that services customers from Sydney to Tokyo, from Frankfurt to San Francisco. What also became evident to us, far beyond our initial business plan, was that we would create a training ecosystem that delivered massive ROI numbers. Producing great results for our customers has ultimately helped our Social Selling Mastery program expand globally in the world's largest companies. Frankly, two guys from small-town Canada just didn't think that big when we started the business.

We didn't wake up one day and just build the Social Selling Mastery program. Heck, this is Version 3.1 and there will be evolving versions every quarter and every year. We had to learn from customer feedback.

We learned very quickly that sales professionals executing on LinkedIn are just a small portion of a social selling ecosystem. Without your company's leadership buy-in and commitment to be accountable to reinforce activity, behavioral change in the long run would just not happen. As we saw customers scale beyond regional offices into other business units and in other countries, empirical data was essential. We spent, and continue to spend, thousands of internal man hours learning various ways to help our customers measure social selling from knowledge transfer to in-market execution. Finally, the biggest revelation hit us in 2013, when we recognized that sales professionals were a portion of the buyer interaction and can only succeed when partnered with marketing. Over the last three years, we've dedicated more man-hours to improving sales and marketing integration than any other element of the Social Selling Mastery program. I truly do believe that social selling is simply the by-product of effective sales and marketing integration. I also believe that solving this challenge will become the most important topic for companies over the next five years. You can bet that we intend to be on the forefront of this Herculean endeavor.

I wanted to write this book because I see too many companies around the world stuck in the proverbial mud. They are running the same sales playbook they've been using since the 1990s and, frankly, they are losing the mindshare of their buyers. Unfortunately, their big-brand vanity blinds them from looking at their sales process objectively. I wanted to offer you a massive time saver as this book will help you accelerate your speed-to-market. We save companies thousands of man hours and millions of dollars so they don't jump off a cliff and start building their parachute on the way down. Save that heartache for entrepreneurs. Oh, and it feels great to make our customers a ton of money in the process.

Finally, I'm so proud of our team at Sales for Life. We are the first sales performance training company anywhere in the world to develop the order of operations needed to scale social selling globally in 90 days. We put together the chess pieces and called the plays to become the grandmasters. That's our value and that's the value I wanted to provide you in this book. Again, I truly feel blessed to be in the right place at the right time to have helped pioneer the social and digital sales world.

Index